RIGHTLY DIVIDING THE
WORD OF TRUTH

RIGHTLY DIVIDING THE
WORD OF TRUTH

A Fresh Perspective to Understanding The Bible

FRED S WOLFE II

WESTBOW
PRESS
A DIVISION OF THOMAS NELSON

WestBow Press books may be ordered through booksellers or by contacting:

WestBow Press
A Division of Thomas Nelson
1663 Liberty Drive
Bloomington, IN 47403
www.westbowpress.com
1-(866) 928-1240

ISBN: 978-1-4497-4933-0 (sc)
ISBN: 978-1-4497-4931-6 (hc)
ISBN: 978-1-4497-4932-3 (e)

Library of Congress Control Number: 2012907312

Printed in the United States of America

WestBow Press rev. date: 06/22/2012

DEDICATION

I would like to dedicate this book to my beautiful and virtuous wife of 33 years, Joanne. She has been by my side through good times and bad. We have done ministry, built a business, and have been in many ventures together. Also to our two sons, David and Jonathan; I am so proud to be their father. We have two beautiful granddaughters, who have won our hearts over, making us proud grandparents. We are looking forward to being in their lives as my grandparents were in mine.

I would also like to dedicate this book to my late grandparents, Beryl Love and George Washington Bristow and Helen Harris and Fredrick Stevenson Wolfe. They played as great a role influencing my life as my parents did.

TABLE OF CONTENTS

Throughout this text, all quotes, unless otherwise noted, are from the King James Version (KJV) of the Bible. I will also be quoting verses from other versions or translations. These will be noted as NRSV, NASU, NASB, etc. The KJV is the most easily referenced and the version upon which Strong's numbering system is based. I will make many references to Strong's numbers, of which there are 8674 Hebrew root words used in the Old Testament and 5624 Greek root words used in the New Testament.

The KJV italicizes words that were added by the translators, but literally hundreds of other words were added, which were not italicized. Since italicized words are used for emphasis in professional writing, I will [bracket] words that have been added by the translators in plain text, so you will know that they do not appear in the original texts. I save italics for my own emphasis upon the quotes examined in this book.

Unfortunately, there is not a Bible in print that shows all of the words the translators added. Any serious student of the Bible must have a computer Bible program in order to know for sure, what has been added and what has not. I will also take the liberty, as other translators have, of changing punctuation and capitalization to portray what I believe to be God's original intent. For example, look at 1 John 5:7–8:

> For there are three that bear record [in heaven, the Father, the
> Word, and the Holy Ghost: and these three are one. And there
> are three that bear witness in earth]: the spirit, and the water,
> and the blood: and these three agree in one.

As you can see, none of the words have been italicized, but the translators added all the words between the brackets. Here is how the NRSV portrays these two verses:

> There are three that testify: the Spirit and the water and the
> blood and these three agree.

If you were used to reading the KJV, you would think that there was something wrong with the NRSV translation. Without access to a program like *Biblesoft's PC Study Bible*, you would not know that the NRSV was actually the more accurate of the two versions.

I will use parentheses to identify the Greek words and to show words I am adding for further clarification. I will only do this in order to attempt to communicate a simpler or more accurate understanding of a given verse.

CHAPTER 1

RIGHTLY DIVIDING
THE WORD OF TRUTH

In order to understand the Word of God, the Bible, it must be "rightly divided." Until you do so, you will never walk in the fullness of the power that is yours. In Paul's second personal epistle to Timothy (2:15), he says,

> Study (exert thyself), to shew thyself approved unto God, a workman that needeth not to be ashamed, rightly dividing the word of truth.

Ortho-tomeo, Handling the Word of God

To *rightly divide* means to dissect correctly, to cut straight. Paul uses the Greek word *orthotomeo* (3718), which comes from the words *orthos* (straight, erect, upright)[1] and *tomoteros* (to cut comprehensibly, decisively).[2] *Tomoteros* is used one other time, in Hebrews 4:12. To picture the meaning of *orthos*, think of an orthodontist as someone who makes one's teeth

---

[1] NT:3718 *orthotomeoo, orthotomoo*; 1. to cut straight; 2. dropping the idea of cutting, to make straight and smooth; 2 Ti 2:15. Thayer's

[2] NT:5114 *tomoteros* (tom-o'-ter-os); comparative of a derivative of the primary temno (to cut; more comprehensive or decisive than NT:2875, as if by a single stroke, whereas that implies repeated blows, like hacking); more keen. Strong's

straight and prevents them from being crooked. For *tomoteros*, think of a butcher separating the different cuts of meat from an animal. *Tomoteros* is differentiated from *koptos* (hacking, chopping).

One of the main reasons why there is so much misunderstanding of God's Word is that there has been a failure to rightly divide the Word, which has been handed down to us through centuries of abuse, private interpretation, and outright fraud. One of the more obvious examples is the separating of the Old and New Testaments between Malachi and Matthew. I will argue that there are logical divisions in the Bible that are applicable to us directly and indirectly. It is easy to see that the *Law of Moses*, and, hence, *The Law Administration*, ends with the fulfillment of the Law in the Gospels of Matthew, Mark, Luke, and John. When one administration ends, another one begins (though not always immediately), until the last administration of the Everlasting Kingdom, where the New Heaven and New Earth will be. We can learn a lot from what was written to those of the Law Administration, which ends with the Gospel of John, but it would be catastrophic to attempt to live by that to which Christ put an end. For example, during the Law Administration, *salvation* was dependant upon one staying faithful to the Law of Moses until the day one died, whereas during this administration—the Grace Administration, which began in Acts 2—salvation is freely given *by grace*, the undeserved divine favor of God.

According to Strong's, the word "dispensation" (*oikonomia*, 3622), which is used in Ephesians 3:2, means "administration as in a religious economy." Thayer's defines it as "the management of a household, specifically, the management, oversight, administration of others' property." Another way of understanding this word is from the viewpoint of governance, *how things are governed*.

The written Word (*logos*) is logical and its divisions are logical. The first dispensation or administration ended with the expulsion of Adam and Eve from the Garden of Eden (Ge 3:24). The second administration ended with the Flood—a very conclusive end! The time that Noah spent in the Ark

is supposed to be like. This is, I believe, *the greatest key to "rightly dividing" the word of truth*, to the point that, the truth, as it is designed to do, will truly set you free.

Take, for example, the word "*disciple(s)*, a learner or pupil." It appears 298 times from Matthew 10:24 to Acts 21:16. After that, the word is never used again. Why do you suppose that is? It is because we are no longer just students of Christ, but sons of God and joint heirs with Jesus Christ. Romans 8:14 says, "For as many as are led by the spirit of God, they are *sons* of God." We are no longer disciples. After Acts 2, the 11 followers Jesus had chosen, plus others, became Apostles, which was one of the gifts Jesus gave after his Ascension. Romans 5 says that we have received "apostleship," not discipleship. This is a marked difference.

More specifically, Galatians 4:4–7 says,

> But when the fullness of the time was come (past tense), God sent
> forth his Son, made (*ginomai*, come into being, into existence)
> of a woman, *made under* [the] *law*, to redeem (pay the ransom
> of) them [that were] under [the] law, that we might receive the
> adoption of *sons*. And because ye are sons, God hath sent forth
> the spirit of his Son into [your] (our) hearts, crying, Abba, Father.
> Wherefore thou art no more a servant (slave), but a son; and if a
> son, then an heir of God through [Christ].

The NRSV finishes this verse "[…] and if a child then also an heir, through God." What a different mindset this gives an individual believer, to go from a slave and disciple to a son. The mindset of the Gospels puts believers back under the Law as slaves, not sons and daughters (2Co 6:18).

Another example of failure to rightly divide the Word of Truth is water baptism. John the Baptist instituted it for Jews, as a sign of *repentance*. In this context, repentance means reversal or turning back again. Jews had (have) something to which to return; Gentiles (unbelievers) have nothing to which to return. The second usage of the word "repentance" is recorded in Matthew 3:11: "I indeed baptize you with water unto repentance: *but* he that cometh after me is mightier [than] I, whose shoes I am not worthy to bear: he shall baptize you with [the] holy ghost (spirit) and [with] fire." *"But"* is a very big little word in the Bible. It sets in contrast that which precedes it with that which follows it. This is exactly what happened on the day of Pentecost (Ac 2). Jesus referred to it as *"the promise of the Father"* and he goes on to say, just prior to his Ascension:

> And, being assembled together with [them], commanded them [that] they should not depart from Jerusalem, but wait for the promise of the Father, which, [saith he], ye have heard of me. For John truly baptized with water; *but* ye shall be baptized with [the] holy ghost (spirit) not many days hence. (Ac 1:4–5)

As it turns out, it was just 10 days later. Jesus commanded them to wait for the promise of the Father. This was not something to be ignored. Yet, many leaders in the Church ignore it today. The result of this promise was the manifestation of the gift of holy spirit: speaking in tongues.

> [There is] *one* body, and *one* Spirit, even as ye are called in *one* hope of your calling; *one* Lord (Jesus Christ), *one* faith, *one* baptism, *one* God and Father of all, who [is] above all, and through all, and in [you] all. (Eph 4:4–6)

Again, water baptism was part of the Law Administration. The baptism of holy spirit is the baptism of the Grace Administration. Spiritually, water baptism does nothing for anyone in this day and age. Paul tells us that there is only one valid baptism, and it is not with water.

The four Gospels fulfilled the Law of Moses and ended the Old Testament, as Jesus fulfilled the Law. The book of Acts serves as a transition period between the Old and New Testaments, from the Law of Moses to the grace of God in Christ Jesus. It was not an easy transition and it is still an ongoing battle, mainly because of the clergy's failure to make any attempt to *rightly divide* the word of truth. The Christian Church would be very different, if, when the Bible was first printed, the book of Romans was the first book in the New Testament.

KJV it is translated as, "to heal, preserve, save (self), do well, be (make) whole."

As you can see from these definitions, there are benefits to salvation here and now, as well as in the future. Sometimes it is referred to as the "Promise of Salvation," because its full benefits will not be manifested until after the Gathering Together of the Church and "the Redemption of the purchased possession" (Eph 1:14). The redemption of our lives is explained thusly: we were born as slaves to sin and were (are) being held as ransom by the god of this age, Satan (2Co 4:4). Jesus Christ paid the price of the ransom by offering his own life for ours, so that we could be *redeemed.*

Two other words you may be familiar with are "born again." In Greek, these two words are represented by the compound word, *anagennao. Ana* (303) means up, upward; it denotes repetition, renewal, anew, over again. *Gennao* (1080) is one of the words that is used to describe the birth of our Lord Jesus, as well as everyone else who has been born or begotten. It means to procreate and, metaphorically, to engender, cause to arise. It is translated as "begat," "should be born," "were born," "been born," "shall bear," "bear," "brought forth," "be born (again)," "was born" (Moses), "is delivered," "is born," "free born" (Paul), "is begotten" (us), etc. In 1 John 5:1, *gennao* is used three times and translated in three different ways: "born," "begat," and "begotten."

> [Forasmuch] As ye know that ye were not *redeemed* with corruptible things, [as] silver and gold, from your vain conversation [received] by tradition from your fathers, *but* with the precious blood of Christ, as of a lamb without blemish and without spot, who verily was foreordained before the foundation of the world, but was manifest in these last times for you, who by him do trust in God, who raised him up from the dead, and gave him glory; that your faith and hope might be in God. [Seeing] ye have purified (Sanctify) your souls in obeying the truth [through the Spirit] unto unfeigned love of the brethren; [see that ye] love one another with a pure heart fervently: Being *born again* (*anagennao*, 313), not of corruptible *seed* (*spora*, 4701), but of *incorruptible*, by [the] word, *logos*, of

God, [which] liveth and abideth [for ever] (living and abiding).
(1Pe 1:18–23)

To become born again is not a physical experience; it is a spiritual one. It is not according to the definition of *ana*, but what it denotes: being born anew, getting a new lease on life, so to speak. When a person "gets born again," there is nothing that permanently changes on the outside; it's an inside job. Seed (*spora*) is created within us, making us a new creation. Like all seed, it needs to be watered and nourished to grow into what it is designed to be. Unfortunately, this is something we must do and do according to that which is written directly to us. We will see that this seed is the beginning of the *new* man. Subsequently, the *old* man must be *put off* and this new man must be *put on*. This takes a lot of effort on our part. You can read about this in Galatians 3. It is a part of the "renewed mind" process spoken of in Romans 12:2. You will not read anything about it in Matthew, Mark, Luke, or John.

The key to becoming born again is *hearing* the Word of Truth and *believing* in Jesus Christ. Ephesians 1:13 says, "In him (Christ), you also, when you had *heard* the word of truth, the gospel of your salvation, and had *believed* in him, were marked with the seal of the promised holy spirit" (NRSV). To set a seal upon something or someone implies that something is being sealed inside. 2 Corinthians is more specific: "Now he which stablisheth us with you in Christ, and hath *anointed* us, [is] God; who hath also *sealed* (*sphragizo*, 4972) us, and given the earnest (*arrhabon*, 728) *of the spirit* in our hearts" (1:21–22).[2] The *arrhabon*, of Hebrew origin, is exactly like the earnest money given in a real estate transaction: a pledge of good faith, of more to come. In this case, it is the gift of holy spirit, not money. It represents the down payment on our inheritance, as Ephesians 1:14 says.

---

[2]   I would like to point out that all of us "in Christ" are *anointed*. There is no other anointing in the Church today. No one is any more or less anointed, with the exception of Jesus Christ. No teaching or preaching is specifically anointed. This attitude, which prevails in the Church today, is not only false, but alienating.

Prior to Pentecost, Jesus related this promised gift of holy spirit to *water*, living water.[3]

> In the last day, that great [day] of the feast, Jesus stood and cried, saying, If any man *thirst*, let him come unto me, and *drink*. He that *believeth* on me, as the scripture hath said, out of his belly shall flow rivers of living *water*. (But this spake he of *the spirit*, which they that *believe* on him should receive: for [the Holy] Ghost (spirit) was not yet [given,] because [that] Jesus was not yet glorified). (Jn 7:37–39)

The full measure of spirit was not yet given, unconditionally, as it was on the day of Pentecost.

> Jesus answered and said unto her, Whosoever drinketh of this water shall thirst again: but whosoever drinketh of the water that I shall give him shall never thirst; but the water that I shall give him shall be in him a well of water springing up into everlasting life. (Jn 4:13–14)

When a person *believes on or in Jesus Christ*, they will receive the spirit of God. Holy spirit is the essence of what God is: holy and spirit. The incorruptible seed that God creates in us is *eternal*, because it is incorruptible! Life is in the seed and, in this case, as well as in Mary's case, a new man is *created*: one physically and another spiritually. Ephesians 4:24 says, "And [that] ye put on *the new man*, which after God is created in righteousness and true holiness." Colossians 3:9–10 says, "Lie not one to another, [seeing that] ye have *put off* the old man with his deeds; And have *put on* the new [man,] which is *renewed* in knowledge after [the] image of him that created him." In this case, the image of God is spirit (Jn 4:24).

---

[3] Mark H. Graeser, John A. Lynn, and John W. Schoenheit, *The Gift of the Holy Spirit: Every Christian's Divine Deposit* (Indianapolis: Christian Educational Services, 2006), 71.

No birth can be achieved without conception and conception can only be realized by seed, whether it is physical or spiritual. In our case, those of us who are born again, it was spiritual. In the case of our Lord, Jesus Christ, it was physical. God created the spiritual seed in us and the physical seed in Mary, to beget a new man, a new creation. 2 Corinthians 5:17 says, "Therefore if any man [be] in Christ, [he is] a new creation: old things are passed away; behold, [all things] are become (*ginomai,* 1096) new." *Ginomai* is a birth word. It is related to the word *gennao*, as in *anagennao*. We will examine these words later in more detail, but here you can see that in Christ Jesus a fresh, new start is granted to believers. Fresh starts imply clean slates and, thus, we have the opportunity to rewrite our own history!

> Blessed [be,] the God and Father of our Lord Jesus Christ, which according to his abundant mercy *hath begotten* us *again* (*anagennao*), unto a lively hope by [the] resurrection (*anastasis,* raising) of Jesus Christ from [the] dead, to an inheritance incorruptible (*aphthartos,* 862), and undefiled (*amiantos,* 283), and that fadeth not away (*amarantos,* 263), reserved in heaven for you, who are kept by [the] power (*dunamis*) of God through faith *unto salvation* ready *to be*, revealed in [the] last time, (future). (1Pe 1:3–5)

What a mouthful that is! Our inheritance is not heaven itself, but it is reserved there for us, where we will receive it.

In the passage above, *anagennao* is translated as "hath begotten again." In 1 Peter 1:23, it was translated as "being born again." As you can see, *born and begotten* are used interchangeably, but the understanding is the same. No matter how you look at it or choose to translate it, it is a spiritual matter.

A lot happens when you *hear* with your ears, *confess* with your mouth, and *believe* in your heart. This is all that is required to receive the Promise of Salvation. There really are not enough words in my vocabulary to express how generous God is. You are probably thinking, "That can't be all there is to it; that's just too easy." Well, I am glad to tell you that this really is all you have to do to have the Promise of Salvation and an inheritance reserved for you in heaven. This is empowering knowledge! You should be jumping off your seat to know this; this is what the Word of God says about itself. It is its own witness. And you really can take this to the bank!

What you do not have to do is confess all your sins. There is no way anyone could ever remember them all anyway! Even if you could, what would happen if you forgot one? Instead, we confess the Saviour, the Lord Jesus Christ, and our sins are wiped away. We receive a clean slate, a fresh start! The confession of sin does not come into play until *after* you are born again; after you become a new creation in Christ; after you have established *fellowship* with the Father and the Lord Jesus Christ.

> If we say that we have *fellowship* with him, and walk in darkness, we lie, and do not the truth: but if we walk in the light, as he is in the light, we have fellowship one with another, and the blood of Jesus [Christ] his Son cleanseth us from all sin. If we say that we have no sin, we deceive ourselves, and the truth is not in us. If we *confess* our sins, he is faithful and just to *forgive* us [our] sins, and to *cleanse* us from all unrighteousness. If we say that we have not sinned, we make him a liar, and his word is not in us. (1Jn 1:6–10)

Attributes of Salvation

Let us look back at some of the words used in conjunction with being born again:

1. "Not of corruptible seed, but of *incorruptible* (*afthartos*, 862)," imperishable, immortal.[4] Unable to rot, decay or die. (1Pe 1:23)
2. "Which liveth and abideth *forever*" inside you! It cannot be removed! (1Pe 1:23)

---

[4] See Thayer's.

3. "According to his abundant *mercy* (4183, 1656)." (1Pe 1:3)
4. "Unto a lively *hope* (*zao elpis*, 2198, 1680)," the hope of his return for us. (1Pe 1:3)
5. "By the raising again of Jesus Christ." (1Pe 1:4)
6. "To an *inheritance* incorruptible (862) and undefiled (*amiantos*, 283)." (1Pe 1:4)
7. "That fadeth not away (*amarantos*. 263)." (1Pe 1:4)
8. "*Reserved in Heaven* for YOU!" (1Pe 1:5)
9. "Who are kept (*phroureo*, 5432)," guarded or protected. (1Pe 1:5)
10. "By the power (*dunamis,* 1411, miraculous power, strength, ability) of God." (1Pe 1:5)
11. "Through faith *unto salvation* (4102, 1519, 4991)." (1Pe 1:5)
12. "ready (2092, prepared) to be revealed, in the last time (*apokalupto*, 601)." (1Pe 1:5)

Does God pull any punches? Does He leave room for any doubt? Does He mean what He says and say what He means? Could He possibly be any clearer as to His intentions? How simple can He get?

CHAPTER IV

OF JEWISH SALVATION

Ye worship ye know not what: we know what we worship: for
salvation is of the Jews. (Jn 4:22)

Salvation in Israel

Salvation is not something peculiar to the Christian Church. YHWH is
the author of salvation and it is something that he has always represented.
It is a common theme from Genesis 49:18 to Revelation 19:21. The word
is used 119 times in the Old Testament and 45 times in the New. Two
words from the New Testament and four words from the Old are translated
as "salvation." The common denominator of all these words' meanings is
something like *saved, deliverance, victory, rescue, or safety.* Let us look at a
few verses from the Old Testament:

> And Moses said unto the people, Fear ye not, stand still, and
> *see the salvation* of Yahweh, which he will *shew* to you to day:
> for the Egyptians whom ye have seen to day, ye shall see them
> again no more for ever. Yahweh shall fight for you, and ye shall
> hold your peace. (Ex 14:13–14)

> Yahweh [is] my strength and song, and he is become my
> salvation: he is my God, and I will prepare him an habitation;

my father's God, and I will exalt him. Yahweh is a man of war:
Yahweh is his name. (Ex 15:2–3)

But Jeshurun waxed fat, and kicked: thou art waxen fat, thou
art grown thick, thou hast grown fat; then he forsook God
who made him, and despised the refuge of his salvation. (Dt
32:15)

And Saul said, There shall not a man be put to death this
day: for to day Yahweh hath wrought salvation in Israel. (1Sa
11:13)

And David spake unto Yahweh the words of this song in the
day that Yahweh had delivered him out of the hand of all his
enemies, and out of the hand of Saul: and he said, Yahweh my
security, and my *stronghold*, and my *deliverer*; the God of my
refuge; in him will I trust: my *protector*, and the power of my
salvation, my high place, and my retreat, my safety; thou savest
me from injustice. I will call on Yahweh, worthy to be praised:
so shall I be *saved* from mine enemies. (2Sa 22:1–4)

In verse 3 of the latter quotation, "salvation" is *yesha'* (3468) and
"safety," "savest," and "saved" (verse 4) are all *yasha'* (3467). As you can see,
for Israel, salvation originated with Yahweh. As it is with Christians today,
salvation was not just something *to come*. It was and is a current state of
peace, derived from knowing who Yahweh—our salvation, our deliverer,
our refuge, our stronghold and our protector—is. He has not changed.
There is a great deal of security and peacefulness in knowing that you have
the Promise of Salvation.

The first usage of the word "salvation" in what is known as the New
Testament (but which is in actuality the end of the Old), is in Luke 1:69,
in a passage about John the Baptist:

And his father Zacharias was filled with [the] holy ghost (spirit),
and prophesied, saying: Blessed [be the] Lord God of Israel; for

he hath visited and redeemed his people, and hath raised up an horn of *salvation* for us in [the] house of his servant David; As he spake by [the] mouth of his holy prophets, which [have been] since [the] world [began: That] we should be *saved* from our enemies, and from [the] hand of all that hate us; to perform [the] mercy [promised] to our fathers, and to remember his holy covenant; [the] oath which he sware to our father Abraham, [that] he would grant unto us, [that] we being delivered out of [the] hand of our enemies, might serve him without fear, in holiness and righteousness before him all the days of our [life.] And thou, child, shalt be called [the] prophet of the Highest: for thou shalt go before (the sight) [the face] of the Lord (God) to prepare his ways; to give knowledge of *salvation* unto his (God's) people by [the] remission of their sins. (Lk 1:67–77)[1]

The second place salvation is mentioned is in Luke 2:30, which concerns John's cousin, Jesus:

And when the days of her purification (40 days), *according to the law of Moses* were accomplished, they brought him to Jerusalem, to present [him] to the Lord (*YHWH*) as it is written in [the] law of the Lord, every male that openeth [the] womb shall be called holy to the Lord; and to offer a sacrifice according to that which is said in the law of the Lord, A pair of turtledoves, or two young pigeons. And, behold, there was a man in Jerusalem, whose name was Symeon; and the same man [was] just and devout, waiting for [the] consolation of Israel: and [the] holy ghost (spirit) was *upon* him. And it was revealed (*chrematizo*) unto him by the Holy Ghost, that he should not see death, before he had seen the Lord's (Yahweh's) Christ. And he came by *the spirit* into the temple and when the parents brought in the child Jesus, to do for him after the custom of the law, he took him up in his arms, and blessed God, and said, Lord, now lettest thou thy servant depart in peace, according to thy word:

---

[1]   In this passage, the object of salvation is Israel.

For mine eyes have *seen thy salvation,* that thou hast prepared before the face of all people; a light to lighten (*apokalupsis*) [the] Gentiles, and [the] glory of thy people Israel. And his father [Joseph] and mother marveled at those things which were spoken of him. And Symeon blessed them, and said unto Mary his mother, Behold, this [child] is destined for [the] fall (downfall) and rising again (*anastasis*) of many in *Israel*; and for a sign which shall be spoken against; (yea, a sword shall pierce through thy own soul also,) in order that [the] thoughts of many hearts may be revealed (*apokalupto*). And there was [one] Anna, a prophetess, [the] daughter of Phanuel, of [the] tribe of Aser: She was of a great age, [and] had lived with an husband seven years from her virginity and she [was] a widow until fourscore [and] four years, who departed not [from] the temple, [but] served [God] (ministering) with fastings and prayers night and day. And she coming in that instant gave thanks likewise unto God (*Theos*), and spake of him to all them that looked for *redemption* [in] Jerusalem. (Lk 2:22–38)

As you can see, Joseph and Mary adhered to the Law of Moses. It was the law to which they subjected their son. There are many important things to see in the passage above. First, we have a man whose name is Symeon, who "happened" to be in the temple at the same time as Joseph and Mary. He was not a priest or a rabbi, but he was just and devout and waiting for the solace of Israel. Because of his character, Yahweh had chosen to place *spirit* upon Symeon and reveal to him—by the spirit upon him—that he would not die until he had seen Yahweh's Christ. In those days, holy spirit was available, depending upon certain conditions of character. In his submission to that spirit, Symeon was directed into the temple, where he ran right into Jesus. There must have been hundreds, if not thousands of people there and it was not likely that Symeon knew what Joseph and Mary looked like. This was an incredible moment for Symeon. Imagine the scene: a perfect stranger walks up to you and your wife and takes your 1- or 2-month-old baby out of your arms, declaring "Jesus Yahweh's salvation!"

Symeon told of how Yahweh had prepared Jesus as the salvation of all people, including Gentiles, and the *glory* (kingly majesty of the Messiah) *of Israel!*

The Messiah, Israel's Salvation

Then we see Anna, a woman whose character was deserving of a prophetess. She served in the temple continually after her husband's death and she just "happened" to come by Joseph and Mary at that instant. She too gave thanks to God and spoke of Jesus *as the redemption* they had been waiting for. He was, after all, Yahweh's salvation, according to the words of Symeon. In this passage, the Lord God of Israel communicates by way of or via His spirit to a Jewish man and woman, who had already heard prophesies concerning what manner of person this 40-day-old baby was going to be.

The next use of the word "salvation" is in Luke 19:

> And [Jesus] entered [and] passed through Jericho. And, behold, [there was] a man named Zacchaeus, which was [the] chief among the publicans (tax collectors), and he [was] wealthy. And he sought to see Jesus who he was; and could not for the press, because he was little of stature. So he ran before, [and] climbed up into a sycamore tree to see him: for he was to pass that [way].[2] And when Jesus came to the place, he looked up, [and saw him and] said unto him, Zacchaeus, make haste, [and] come down; for today I must abide at thy house. So he made haste, came down, and received him joyfully. And when they saw [it,] they all murmured, saying, that he was gone to be guest with a man [that is] a sinner.[3] And Zacchaeus stood, [and] said unto the Lord; Behold, Lord, the half of my goods I give to the poor; and

---

[2] Pigs were fed with the fruit of that tree. For him to climb up in it showed great humility for a Jew.

[3] The murmurers are a good example of the religious. They judged Zacchaeus unworthy and sinful, because of his profession, but they failed to take account of his character.

if I have taken any thing [from] any man by false accusation, I restore [him] fourfold. And Jesus said unto him, this day is *salvation* come to this house, forsomuch as he also is a son of Abraham. For the Son of man is come to seek and *to save* that who would otherwise perish. (1–10)

The scene leading up to the next usage of the word "salvation," begins in Acts 3, after Peter heals a man who was lame from birth:

And when Peter saw [it], he answered unto the people, *Ye men of Israel*, why marvel ye at this? or why look ye so earnestly [on] us, as though by our own power or holiness we had made this man to walk? The God of Abraham, and of Isaac, and of Jacob, the God of our fathers, hath glorified *his Son Jesus*; whom ye delivered up, and denied him in [the] presence of Pilate, when he was determined to let him go. But ye denied the Holy One and [the] Just, and desired a murderer to be granted unto you; and killed the Prince of Life, whom God hath raised from [the] dead; whereof we are witnesses. And his name *through faith in his name* hath made this man (person) strong, whom ye see and know: yea, the faith which [is] by him hath given him this perfect soundness in the presence of you all. And now, brethren, I know that through ignorance ye did it, as [did] also your rulers. But those things, which God before had shewed by [the] mouth of all his prophets, [that] Christ should suffer, he hath so fulfilled. *Repent ye therefore, and be converted,* that your sins may be blotted out, when the times of refreshing shall come from the presence of the Lord; and he shall send Jesus Christ, which before was preached unto you: whom the heaven [must] receive until [the] times of restitution of all things (in the future, not now) which God hath spoken by the mouth [of all] his holy prophets since [the] world began. [For] Moses truly said [unto the fathers,] a prophet shall [the] Lord your God raise up unto you of your brethren, like unto me; him shall ye hear in all things whatsoever he shall say unto you. And it shall come to pass, [that] every soul, which will not hear that prophet, shall be destroyed from among the people.

> Yea, and all the prophets from Samuel and those that follow after,
> as many as have spoken, have likewise foretold of these days. *Ye*
> *are the children of the prophets, and of the covenant* which God
> made with our fathers, saying unto Abraham, *in thy seed* shall all
> the kindreds of the earth be blessed, unto you first, God, having
> raised up his Son [Jesus,] *sent him to bless you,* in turning away
> every one [of you] from his iniquities. (12–26)

Then the religious leaders came questioning Peter about the power by
which he healed the man. In whose name had he performed such acts?
Acts 4:8–12 says,

> Then Peter, filled with [the] Holy Ghost (holy spirit), said unto
> *them,* Ye rulers of the people, and elders [of Israel], if we this day
> be examined of [the] good deed done to the impotent man, by
> "what means" (this certain one) he is made whole, be it known
> unto you all, and *to all the people of Israel,* that by the name of
> Jesus Christ of Nazareth, whom ye crucified, whom God raised
> from [the] dead, [even] by him doth this man stand here before
> you whole. This is *the stone* which was set at nought of you
> builders, which is become [the] head of the corner. Neither is
> there salvation_in any other: *for there is none other name under*
> *heaven given among men, whereby we must be saved.*

Peter was a Jew and he was speaking to Jews, the seed of Abraham.
The "times of refreshing and restitution," along with everything else I have
discussed thus far, are foremostly for or addressed to Israel. This *is* the will
of Yahweh for the Jews. These passages about the salvation of Israel have
brought us to this point. All of your prophets have declared that Jesus
Christ is God's plan for salvation.

Paul's Prayer to God for Israel

There are many other verses on salvation that concern Israel, but I
am going to close this chapter with the apostle Paul, who was a "Hebrew

of Hebrews (Jew of Jews), of the tribe of Benjamin and concerning righteousness according to the law: blameless" (Php 3:5). In the first doctrinal epistle to the church, Paul says,

> Brethren, my heart's desire and prayer to God *for Israel* is, that they might be *saved*. For I bear them record that they have a zeal of God, but not according to knowledge. For they being ignorant of *God's righteousness,* and going about to establish *their own* righteousness, have not submitted themselves unto the righteousness of God. For Christ is *the end of the law* for righteousness to every one that believeth. For Moses describeth the righteousness which is of the law, That the man which doeth those things shall live by them. But the righteousness which is of faith speaketh on this wise, Say not in thine heart, Who shall ascend into heaven? [...] Or, Who shall descend into the deep? [...] but what saith it? The word is nigh thee, even in thy mouth, and in thy heart: that is, the word of faith, which we preach; that if thou shalt confess with thy mouth the Lord Jesus, and shalt believe in thine heart that God hath raised him from the dead, thou shalt be *saved*. For with the heart man believeth *unto righteousness*; and with the mouth confession is made *unto salvation*. For the scripture saith, 'Whosoever believeth on him *shall not be ashamed*. For there is no difference between the Jew and the Greek: for the same Lord over all is rich unto all that call upon him. For whosoever shall call upon the name of the Lord shall be saved. (Ro 10:1–13)

Whosoever means anyone: Jew, Muslim, Buddhist, and all other Gentiles of every race, color, or creed. It is all-inclusive, not exclusive. It is Yahweh's will that all men be saved and come unto a full knowledge of the truth: "Who will have all men to be *saved*, and to come unto *the* knowledge of *the* truth. For there is one God, and one mediator between God and men, *the man* Christ Jesus" (1Ti 2:4–5). God does not want anyone to miss this boat. The number one thing that will keep you from it is *pride*, thinking more highly of yourself than you ought to or, as my father would say, "too much for your own good." There was a time when salvation was only for Israel. We should not allow anything to keep us from this opportunity of a lifetime.

CHAPTER V

PAUL'S DOCTRINE: THE GOSPEL OF GOD IN CHRIST JESUS

The Authority of the Apostle Paul

Romans is the first doctrinal epistle written *to* the Church to which all born again, saved believers belong. It only makes sense that with the end of the administration of the Law of Moses, a new doctrine (*didaskalia,* instruction, the function or the information; teaching)[1] of correct believing be established. At the beginning of the book Romans, Paul establishes his authority, as he does at the outset of most of his other letters to the Church.

> Paul, a servant of Jesus Christ, *called* [to be] *an apostle,* separated unto [the] *gospel of God,* (Which he had promised afore by his prophets in the [holy] scriptures,) concerning his Son [Jesus Christ our Lord] who was *made, (ginomai,* to come into existence) of [the] *seed (spermatos)* of David according to [the] *flesh,* [and] declared [to be the] Son of God with power, according to [the] spirit of holiness, by [the] resurrection (standing up again) from the dead: by whom we have received

---

[1] Strong's NT:1319.

grace and apostleship, for obedience to the faith among all nations, for his name, among whom are ye also [the] called of Jesus Christ. (Ro 1:1–6)

Whenever there is a parenthesis, as in the figure of speech that explains the context, pay close attention.[2] Then, to gain continuity, read the passage again, skipping the parenthesis. We can see here that God previously promised His Gospel through the prophets, which had not come into fruition up to this point in time.

In the second chapter of Romans, Paul speaks about a future judgement in which the secrets of men will be judged according to his (Paul's) Gospel. Be mindful of the usage of "according to," which means in alignment with.

> For as many as have sinned without law shall also perish without law; and as many as have sinned in *the* law shall be judged, by the law, in the day when, [in the future,] God shall judge the secrets of men by Jesus Christ *according to my gospel.* (parenthesis removed) (Ro 2:12, 2:16)

As Paul began Romans, he ends it:

> Now to him, (God) that is of power to stablish you *according to* my gospel, and the preaching of Jesus Christ, *according to* the revelation of the mystery (secret), which was kept secret, since the world began, but now is made manifest, and by the scriptures of the prophets, according to commandment of the everlasting God, made known to all nations *for the obedience of faith* (not the faith of Abraham, but Jesus Christ, according to Paul's Gospel). To God only wise, [be] glory through Jesus Christ for ever. Amen. (Ro 16:25–27)

---

[2] Bullinger, *The Companion Bible,* appendix 6, page 11.

The subject of the preceding verse is our establishment in the revelation of Paul's Gospel. The archaic verb *stablish* derives from the word *sterizo (stay-rid'-zo)*, to set fast, i.e. (literally) *to turn resolutely in a certain direction.* We know that Paul's Gospel is new, because it is "*according to* revelation of the Secret (*musterion*), which was kept secret from the beginning of the world."

> How that by revelation he made known *unto me* the Secret (*musterion*) which [in] other ages was not made known unto the sons of men, as it is now revealed unto his holy apostles and prophets by [the] Spirit; (*by spirit*) that the Gentiles should be *fellowheirs,* and *of the same body,* and *partakers* of his promise in Christ by the gospel. (Eph 3:3, 3:5–6)[3]

Paul was the first one to whom this revelation was ever made known. Failing to see the significance of this and minimizing it is equivalent to a slap in God's face. This revelation was important enough that God kept it a secret thousands of years. It is a travesty to not give this revelation preeminence in Church Doctrine over everything else that preceded it.

> [Even] the mystery (*musterion*, secret), which *hath been hid* from ages and from generations, but now is made manifest to his saints, to whom God would make known what [is] the riches of the glory of this mystery (secret) among the Gentiles; *which is Christ in you,* the hope of glory. (Col 1:26–27)

We will look at one last verse before we delve deeper into the importance of teaching for rightly believing the doctrine of the apostle Paul: "But I certify you, brethren, that the gospel which was preached by me is not after man, for I neither received it of man, neither was I taught [it,] *but by* [the]

---

[3] The presence or absence of the article "the" should be very apparent. It is properly applied before "Secret" and erroneously supplied before "spirit." Spirit (capital S) is God Himself; spirit with a small "s" is God's gift to believers, which is why, here, spirit should not be capitalized.

which, (who) in his times he shall shew, [who is] the blessed
and only Potentate (Prince), the King of kings, and Lord of
lords, *who only hath immortality,* dwelling in the light which
no man can approach unto; whom no man hath seen, nor
can see: to whom [be] honour and power everlasting. Amen.
(1Timothy 6:11–16)

What is "this commandment" that Paul commands us to keep until
the appearance of the Lord Jesus Christ? This can be discerned by looking
at the "remote context" of 1 Timothy 1:1, 1:3, and 1:5, where the "charge"
of verse 3 is "that they teach no other doctrine." I think it is necessary to
take a closer look at these words, because even though some are translated
the same, they are not the same Greek words.

1. "Commandment," in 1Timothy 1:1, is *epitage* (2003), an injunction
    or decree; by implication, authoritativeness.[4]
2. "Charge," in 1 Timothy 1:3, is *paraggello* (3853),[5] which is
    subsequently used in verses 4:11, 5:7, 6:13, and 6:17.
3. In 1Timothy 1:5, "charge" is *paraggelia* (3852),[6] a mandate; also
    in verse 1:18.
4. In 1Timothy 6:14, "commandment" (*entole,* 1785),[7] an order,
    command, charge, or precept.

For those of you who may not know it, Paul was a Hellenistic Jew and,
as such, among other things, he spoke Greek fluently and had an exceptional

---

[4] NT:2003 *epitage* (ep-ee-tag-ay'); from NT:2004; an injunction or decree; by
    implication, authoritativeness. Strong's
[5] NT:3853 *paraggello* (par-ang-gel'-lo); from NT:3844 and the base of NT:32; to
    transmit a message, i.e. (by implication) to enjoin. Strong's
[6] NT:3852 *paraggelia* (par-ang-gel-ee'-ah); from NT:3853; a mandate. Strong's
[7] NT:1785 *entolee, entolees, hee*; an order, command, charge, precept; 1. universally,
    a charge, injunction: Lk 15:29; 2. a commandment; a. universally, Heb 7:16; b.
    ethically: what God prescribes in the law of Moses, Mt 15:3; of the precepts of
    Jewish tradition: Tit 1:14; universally, of the commandments of God, especially
    as promulgated in the Christian religion: 1 Jn 3:23. Thayer's

command of the language. To communicate the importance of what he had to say to Timothy, Paul used five different Greek words. He left no room for misunderstanding. Here is a little more background on Paul:

> But Paul said, I am a man [which am] a Jew of Tarsus, [a city] in Cilicia, a citizen of no mean city: and, I beseech thee, suffer me to speak unto the people. (Ac 21:39)

> The answer of the apostle (remarks Humphry) to the two questions of the Roman captain is such as to show at once that he could speak Greek with elegance, and that he was entitled, to respectful treatment. The word rendered "citizen" [politees] (he adds), implying the possession of civil rights, is emphatic and appropriate; for Tarsus was a free city, having received its liberty from Mark Antony. It was "no mean city," for it enjoyed the title of metropolis of Cilicia, which, together with other privileges, was conferred on it by Augustus. Strabo, in his interesting account of Tarsus, says it surpassed even Athens and Alexandria in its zeal for philosophy, differing from those great schools in one respect-that its students were all natives, and it was not resorted to by foreigners. The natives, however, were not content with a home education, but went abroad to complete their studies, like Paul (Ac 22:3), and often did not return. Rome was full of them. Tarsus derived its civilization, and indeed its origin, from Greece, having been rounded, as its mythology shows, by an Argine colony.[8]

Paul was obviously a highly educated person. In 2 Timothy 1:11, Paul says that he was "appointed, ordained, to be *a herald*, of the divine truth, *an apostle*, one sent forth with orders *and a teacher*" of doctrine. This verse shows us that one may have more than one of the equipping ministries mentioned in Ephesians 4:11. In 2 Timothy 1:13, Paul exhorts us to "Hold

---

[8] "Jamieson, Fausset, and Brown Commentary," Jamieson, Fausset, and Brown Commentary, Electronic Database. Copyright © 1997, 2003, 2005, 2006 by Biblesoft, Inc. All rights reserved.).

fast (stick like glue) to the example of sound words (those true in doctrine), which we have heard of him."

2 Timothy 3 begins by describing the traits of the type of people that you do not want to have anything to do with. Verses 1–8 mention several types, but I will only list some of them:

1. *False accusers,* prone to slander, like Satan, persecuting good men.
2. *Despisers* of those who are good, hostile to virtue, oppose goodness.
3. *Traitors,* those who betray one another, like Judas.
4. Those having a form, *morphosis,* appearance of godliness, but contradicting the power thereof.

In 2 Timothy 3:10, Paul gives a few of his own characteristics to Timothy when he says, "But thou hast *fully known (parakoloutheo)* my doctrine, manner of life, purpose, faith, longsuffering, charity, patience, persecutions (and) afflictions." Indeed, Timothy had an intimate, side-by-side relationship with Paul, as the word *parakoloutheo* implies. Timothy knew all there was to know about Paul. Paul then exhorts Timothy: "But continue thou in the things which thou hast *learned* and hast been assured of, *knowing of whom thou hast learned* [them]" (2Ti 3:14). It is obvious that it was unto Timothy that Paul chose to pass his "torch." The goal of every leader should be to properly replace themselves; not self-perpetuity! When leaders today make it to the "top," they do everything they can to stay there, instead of finding people like Timothy to take their place.

Paul's Final Commandment to Leaders

In 2 Timothy 4:1, Paul delivers his final "charge" to Timothy and to us, as leaders. This "charge" is the strongest of all: *diamarturomai,* to protest earnestly, hortatively, to solemnly affirm:[9]

---

[9] NT:1263 *diamarturomai*; to call gods and men to witness; 1. to testify, i.e. earnestly, religiously to charge: followed by an imperative: Ac 2:40; 2. to attest, testify to, solemnly affirm: Ac 20:23. Thayer's

I *charge* [thee therefore] before God, and [the Lord] Jesus Christ, who shall judge [the] quick (living) and [the] dead [at] his appearing and his kingdom; Preach the word (*logos*); be instant in season (at hand opportunely), out of season (inopportunely); reprove (admonish), rebuke (censure), exhort (encourage, console, strengthen, instruct, teach*) with all longsuffering and doctrine.* For [the] time will come when *they will not endure sound doctrine*; but after their own lusts shall they heap to themselves teachers, having itching ears; (only want to hear the latest gossip) and *they shall turn away* [their] *hearing from the truth,* and shall be turned unto fables (myths). But watch thou in all things, endure afflictions, do [the] work of an evangelist, make full proof of thy ministry. (1–5)

Take a minute and look at the gravity of this charge, as Paul brings *judgment* center stage. He specifies the Judgment at Christ's appearing, when he will come to gather together the Church, beginning his Kingdom, 7 years after the Great Tribulation, at the Sheep and Goat Judgment and the Resurrection (raising) of the Just. It is a sobering reminder that even though those of us who are saved are sealed, we will all be judged at the Judgment Seat of Christ. It will be too late to change anything after his appearance. The Church thinks they have something to do with Christ's return for them. They think they have to fulfill the Great Commission before Christ can come back for them. They think that Christ's appearing is somehow conditional upon something they must do. These suppositions are the manifestations of wrongly dividing the Word of Truth. The Church needs to get their heads screwed on right and start living the Word according to all the *according to's* we have looked at in this chapter. The apostle Peter explained it like this: "For we have not followed cunningly devised fables, when we made known unto you the power and coming of our Lord Jesus Christ, but were eyewitnesses of his majesty" (2Pe 1:16).

Sophisms, Cunningly Devised Fables

Today the Church is following "cunningly devised (*sophizo*, 4679) fables." The word *sophizo* means to render wise; in sinister acceptation, to form "sophisms," continue plausible error.[10] Merriam-Webster defines sophism as "an argument used to deceive, apparently correct in form, but in actuality, invalid." These fables are cunningly devised, such that they are plausible, which, according to the same source, is "worthy of belief, but often specious—having a false look of truth or genuineness."

I touched upon these concepts in the beginning of this chapter, with the mention of *pseudologos*. "Now the Spirit (God) speaketh expressly, that in [the] latter times some shall depart from the faith, giving heed to seducing spirits, and doctrines of devils; *speaking lies* in hypocrisy; having their conscience seared with a hot iron" (1Ti 4:1–2). "Seducing" (*planos*, 4108)[11] is used five times in the New Testament and four of those times it is translated as "deceiver:" Matthew 27:63 alludes to Jesus as a deceiver; 2 Corinthians 6:8 refers to true believers as deceivers; and 2 John 7 uses the word twice: "For many *deceivers* are entered into the world, who confess not [that] Jesus Christ is come in [the] flesh. This is *a deceiver* and *an* antichrist." These "deceivers" are seducing spirits to which believers adhere. These contrary beliefs turn into "doctrines of devils,"[12] speaking lies and *pseudologos,* which is defined as promulgating erroneous Christian doctrine.[13] The verse goes on to say that those who "give heed," apply themselves to these false doctrines, have seared consciences. The phrase "having seared with a hot iron," is one Greek word, *kausteriazo* (NT:2743), from which we get the English word cauterize: to render insensitive. So, in two of the five usages of *planos*, Jesus Christ and the true believers were accused of being the deceivers. Today, Christianity is thoroughly entrenched in pseudo, false, or fraudulent doctrine for faith and practice.

---

[10] NT:4679 *sophizo* (sof-id'-zo); from NT:4680; to render wise; in a sinister acceptation, to form "sophisms," i.e. continue plausible error. Strong's

[11] 4108 *planos* (plan'-os); of uncertain affinity; roving (as a tramp), i.e. (by implication) an impostor or misleader; KJV - deceiver, seducing. Strong's

[12] NT:1140 *daimonion* (dahee-mon'-ee-on); neuter of a derivative of NT:1142; a daemonic being; by extension *a deity*: (god). Strong's

[13] NT:5573 *pseudologos* (psyoo-dol-og'-os); from NT:5571 and NT:3004; mendacious, i.e. promulgating erroneous Christian doctrine. Strong's

This is what God, the Spirit, said would take place and it has continued unto this day. Only now, the arguments for their error are so profound that no one can logically explain them.

When Paul wrote to the Corinthian believers, he encouraged them to remember what he had taught them. He reminded them of who "fathered" them in the Word of Truth:

> For though ye have ten thousand instructors in Christ, yet have *ye not many fathers*: For in Christ Jesus I have begotten you through the gospel. Wherefore I beseech you, *be ye followers of me.* For this cause have I sent unto you Timotheus, who is my beloved son, and faithful in the Lord, *who shall bring you into remembrance of my ways* which be in Christ, as I teach every where in every church. (1Co 4:15–17)

I can see how this statement could be interpreted as being full of pride: "I have begotten you, follow me, remember my ways!" But, Paul says that that these things are in Christ and Christ Jesus, three times! *Remember, do not forget!*

> If thou *put the brethren in remembrance* of these things, thou shalt be a good minister of Jesus Christ, nourished up *in the words of faith and of good doctrine,* whereunto thou hast attained. (1Ti 4:6)

The opposite is true as well: if you *do not* put those whom you oversee in remembrance of these things, you will not be considered a good minister of Jesus Christ and no one will be educated in the words of faith and *good* doctrine.

> Of these things *put them in remembrance,* charging them before God (*Theos*) [the Lord], that they strive not about words to no profit, but to the subverting of the hearers. Study to shew thyself approved unto God, a workman that needeth not to be ashamed, rightly dividing the word of truth. But

shun profane [and] vain babblings: for they will increase unto more ungodliness. And their word will eat as doth a canker: of whom is Hymenaeus and Philetus; Who concerning the truth have erred, saying [that] the resurrection is past already; and overthrow the faith of some. Nevertheless the foundation of God standeth sure, having this seal, [The] Lord knoweth them that are his. And, Let every one that nameth the name of Christ depart from unrighteousness [iniquity]. (2Ti 2:14–19)

"Words to no profit" are not useful or serviceable to the doctrine of godliness. As leaders, we are commanded before God to not argue over unprofitable things. But, the profitable things, that we are to contend for is everything Paul taught, especially that which is mentioned in the first thirteen verses of this chapter. Contrary to rightly dividing the word of truth and the doctrine of godliness, we are to keep away from "profane, vain babblings," which is what Paul describes as the preaching of the false teachers. Whatever was not agreeable to the doctrine of truth was, in the sight of God, empty and profane babbling, engendering nothing but ungodliness, and daily increasing in that.[14]

The Foundation of Jesus Christ

Paul's church epistles represent the foundation of Jesus Christ. In 1 Corinthians 3:10, Paul said that *According to* the grace of God which is given unto me, as a wise masterbuilder, I have laid [the] foundation, and another buildeth thereon. But let every man take heed how he buildeth thereupon." Peter did not lay the foundation; nor did John; neither did Matthew, Mark, or Luke. Paul did, but not of his own accord.

Jesus Christ is referred to as the chief cornerstone of the foundation of God's building (1Co 3:9). What we build in our lives must be built upon the foundation of the resurrected Jesus Christ. 1 Corinthians 3:11 says,

---

[14] "Adam Clarke's Commentary," Electronic Database. Copyright © 1996, 2003, 2005, 2006 by Biblesoft, Inc. All rights reserved.)_____

"For other foundation can no man lay than that is laid, which is Jesus Christ." Verses 3:8–15 speak about "rewards" (*misthos*), which means dues paid for work; wages or hire.[15] It is used 29 times in the New Testament. It is very important to understand what the foundation of Jesus Christ is, because otherwise, everything you build in this life, for the glory of God, could be destroyed when it is tested with fire at the Judgment Seat of Christ. 1 Corinthians 3 actually says, you "will suffer loss;" you will lose *the reward* you would have received:

> Now, (But) if any man build upon this foundation gold, silver, precious stones, wood, hay, stubble—every man's work shall be made manifest: for the day shall declare it, because it shall be revealed by fire; and the fire shall try every man's work of what sort it is. If any man's work abide which he hath built thereupon, he shall receive *a reward*. If any man's work shall be burned, he shall *suffer loss* (injury, damages): but he himself shall be saved; yet so as by fire. (12–15)

For the born-again believer, these four scriptures could very well be the most important verses in this book. What you believe matters. Rewards are something you earn after you become a son of God; they are the results of faithfulness to God's rightly divided Word. Everything we say, think, or do, affects others. This is why Paul stresses the relevance of our representation in 1 Corinthians 3:16–17. Here, he refers to the Church as a whole, as the Temple of God.[16] We belong to and are an integral part of the Temple of God. In verse 17, we see what happens to those who defile (or corrupt) the Temple (the Church) with wrong doctrine and error. To emphasize that Paul is talking about many, not just one, he uses the same

---

[15] Thayer's NT:3408.

[16] As indicated by "*ye are* (*este*)," the second person plural present indicative of *eim*. NT:2075 *este* (es-teh'); second person plural present indicative of NT:1510; *ye are*. Strong's

word "ye are (*este*)." Individuals are not the Temple, but individuals make up the Temple.

The word *defile* is also used in 2 Corinthians 11:3–4:

> But I fear, lest by any means, as the serpent beguiled Eve through his subtilty, [so] your minds *should be corrupted* from the simplicity that [is] in Christ. For if he that cometh preacheth another Jesus, whom we have not preached, or if ye receive another spirit, which ye have not received, *or another gospel*, which ye have not accepted, ye might well bear with (you hold yourself up *against*) [him].

People are not generally deceived into believing error by being beat up with it. Deception is usually accomplished through "subtilty."[17] This word is associated with *sophizo* in the previous section. We should also look at the word "serpent" (covered later in more detail). Figuratively, a serpent is "an artful malicious person, who is sly and cunning."[18] Paul was afraid that people would be beguiled away from the truth of his Gospel.

In Acts 4:10–12, Peter says,

> Be it known unto you all, and to all the people of Israel, that by the name of Jesus Christ of Nazareth, whom ye crucified, whom God raised from [the] dead, [even] by him doth this man stand here before you whole. This is *the stone* (*lithos*) which was set at nought of you builders, which is become [the] *head of the corner*. Neither is there salvation in any other: for there is none other name under heaven given among men, whereby we must be saved.

---

17 NT:3834 *panourgia* (pan-oorg-ee'-ah); from NT:3835; adroitness, i.e. (in a bad sense) trickery or *sophistry*: KJV - (cunning) craftiness, subtilty. Strong's
18 Strong's NT:3789.

The builders rejected the *lithos*, Jesus Christ, who became the chief corner of the foundation. Ephesians 2:20–22 also refers to Jesus Christ as "the chief corner" of the foundation of the apostles and prophets:

> [And] are built upon the foundation of the apostles and prophets, Jesus Christ himself being [the] *chief corner*[stone] in whom all [the] building fitly framed together groweth unto an holy temple in [the] Lord: in whom ye also are builded together for an habitation of God through [the] spirit.

The chief corner is the stone that sets the alignment for the entire foundation. Our lives need to be in alignment with this corner. Collectively, we are all the Temple, while, individually, we are tabernacles for God. "For we know that if our earthly house, residence, of [this] tabernacle[19] were dissolved, we have a building of God, an house not made with hands, eternal in the heavens" (2Co 5:1). Similarly, "Yea, I think [it] meet, as long as I am *in this tabernacle,* to stir you up [by putting you] in remembrance; Knowing that shortly I must put off this *my tabernacle,* even as our Lord Jesus Christ hath shewed me" (2Pe 1:13–14). We can see, from the next verse, that here Peter is talking about dying.

The foundation that we are to be building upon in order to receive the rewards that will not be burnt with fire at the Judgment Seat of Christ, is that of the resurrected Jesus, known as the Lord Jesus, Christ Jesus, Jesus Christ, and the Lord Jesus Christ. Recall 2 Corinthians 11:4: "another Jesus?" Many churches and pastors talk a lot about Jesus without ever mentioning his appellatives. Jesus was never called any of these names in the Gospels, prior to his death. As I have said to my fellow believers many times, there are many Jesuses, but only one Christ. The words "Jesus Christ" are used 196 times in the New Testament, with only four of those references occurring in the Gospels. "Christ Jesus," which is specific to the resurrected Jesus, is used 58 times from Acts 19 to 1 Peter. Together, these

---

[19] NT:4636 *skenos* (skay'-nos); from NT:4633; a hut or *temporary residence,* i.e. *(figuratively) the human body* (as the abode of the spirit). Strong's

two names have spiritual significance. Using the name Jesus constantly and alone has spiritual significance as well, even though there is only a subtle difference.

The best picture of the foundation comes from the revelation that Paul received from Jesus Christ in the Church Epistles, which are written directly to the Church of the Body of Christ, of which we are members, in particular: "Now *ye are* (*este*) [the] body of Christ, and members in particular" (1Co 12:27), with Jesus Christ being the head; "And hath put all [things] under his feet, and gave him [to be the] *head* over all [things] to the church, which is his body, the fulness of him that filleth all in all" (Eph 1:22–23).

Please go back and see all of the times we are exhorted to follow Paul and his Gospel, not because it is his, but because it is really the Gospel of the resurrected Christ and the Gospel of God Almighty. There should be no doubt at all that Paul's Gospel is the true Gospel of Jesus Christ. It is the Gospel that we are to follow in faith and practice.

CHAPTER VI

THE BODY OF CHRIST

When the day of Pentecost had fully come, 50 (hence the prefix *pent-*) days after Jesus Christ rose from the dead, a new Church was born: the Body of Christ. It was born in and of spirit. When the roughly 120 followers of Jesus received the promise of the Father, it manifested itself and they began to speak in languages that they themselves did not know or understand.

The first thing we need to establish is where this occurred and why it could not have occurred where tradition teaches us that it did. We begin in Acts 2:1–2:

> And when the day of Pentecost was fully come, they were all with one accord in one place. And suddenly there came a sound from heaven as of a rushing mighty wind, and it filled all *the house* where they were sitting.

Continually in the Temple

Tradition has it that these 120 people were in someone's upper room, where they slept, changed clothes, etc. Yet, the last verse of Luke says that they "were continually in the temple, praising and blessing God" (Lk 24:53). Undoubtedly, the confusion is caused by a failure to understand the word "house." The temple was referred to as *the house* of God. Furthermore, women would not have been allowed into the quarters where the men were living.

> But he said unto them, Have ye not read what David did, when he was an hungered, and they that [were] with him; How he entered into *the house* of God, and did eat the shewbread. (Mt 12:3–4)

> And Jesus went into *the temple* [of God,] and cast out all them that sold and bought in the temple, and overthrew the tables of the moneychangers, and the seats of them that sold doves, and said unto them, It is written, My (God's) *house* shall be called [the] *house* of prayer; but ye have made it a den of thieves. (Mt 21:12–13)

> And said unto them that sold doves, Take these things hence; make not *my Father's house* an house of merchandise. And his disciples remembered that it was written, The zeal of thine house hath eaten me up. (Jn 2:16–17)

On the other hand, the upper room is where Jesus' 12 Disciples had chosen "abode," i.e. stayed, lived, or resided. It was the top story of a house. This was the Feast of Weeks in Jerusalem, the second of three major Jewish festivals. The city was teeming with people. The upper room was probably filled to capacity with 12 people in it, let alone 120!

The "one accord"[1] of Acts 2:1 and the "one accord"[2] of Acts 1:14 are not the same words. In verse 1:14 it means "of mind," while 2:1, it connotes "place or time." In Acts 1:14, the people were in one accord in prayer, while in 2:1, they were in one accord in the Temple. Acts 2:5–12 continues,

---

[1] NT:3661 *homothumadon* (hom-oth-oo-mad-on'); adverb from a compound of the base of NT:3674 and NT:2372; unanimously: KJV - with one accord *(mind)*. Strong's

[2] NT:3674 *homou* (hom-oo'); genitive case of homos (the same; akin to NT:260) as adverb; *at the same place or time*. Strong's

And there were dwelling at Jerusalem Jews, devout men, out of every nation under heaven. Now when this was noised (voiced) [abroad], the multitude came together, and were perplexed, because [that] *every man heard them speak* in his own language.[3] And they were [all] amazed and marveled, saying [one to another,] Behold, are not all these which speak Galilaeans? And *how hear we every man in our own tongue,* wherein we were born? Parthians, and Medes, and Elamites, and the dwellers in Mesopotamia, and in Judaea, and Cappadocia, in Pontus, and Asia, Phrygia, and Pamphylia, in Egypt, and in the parts of Libya about Cyrene, and strangers of Rome, Jews and proselytes, Cretes and Arabians, *we do hear them speak in our tongues the wonderful works of God.* And they were all amazed, and were in doubt (thoroughly at a loss,) saying one to another, What meaneth this?

What happened that day is what has come to be known as the baptism of holy spirit, the new birth. It was the manifestation of their receiving the gift of holy spirit from the Holy Spirit. It was the external manifestation of the internal dwelling and reality of the spirit of God. Jesus had told them to wait for it at Jerusalem:

And, being assembled together with [them,] commanded them [that] they should not depart from Jerusalem, but wait for *the promise of the Father,* which, [saith he,] ye have heard of me. For John truly baptized with water; but ye shall be baptized with [the] Holy Ghost (holy spirit) not many days hence. (Ac 1:4–5)

The text reads, "but ye shall be baptized with holy spirit (*pneuma hagion*)." This is one of the other big "buts" in the Bible. It does not say "*and* ye shall

---

3   It is completely illogical to think that all these people assembled in the temple heard the Disciples speaking from someone's apartment without an incredible PA system. But, since they were in the temple, it was no problem to hear them.

be baptized with holy spirit." There are not two baptisms in the Church age; there is only one, holy spirit. At that time, the Law Administration was transitioning into to the Grace Administration. John's baptism was of the Law; this one is of the Grace. The phenomena of Pentecost was that the Jews from every nation under heaven understood what the Disciples were saying: "the wonderful, magnificent works of God." What they spoke built God up in their minds; they praised God and everyone understood it.

When Peter had finished telling them the significance of what had happened, they asked Peter what they should do now.

> Then Peter said unto them, Repent (turn back to God,) and be baptized (with holy spirit) every one of you *in the name of Jesus Christ* for [the] remission of sins, and ye shall receive the gift of the Holy Ghost. (Here the article "the" is properly supplied because it is the gift of or from the Holy Spirit that they would receive from God who is Holy and God who is Spirit.) For *the promise* is unto you, and to your children, and to all that are afar off, [even] as many as [the] Lord our God shall call. (Ac 2:38–39)

The promise is still in effect. This was not a one-time action, just for those who would then believe, but it is a promise to all who believe, until the end of this administration, which ends with the Rapture of the Church.

Here it is also significant to note that Peter told them to be baptized in the name of Jesus Christ. Only his name was used for baptism, healing, or casting out devil spirits throughout the book of Acts. And, it was not just Jesus, but Jesus Christ.

The Church of the One Body

In the first doctrinal epistle written to the Church of God, Romans, it says, "For as we have many members in *one body*, and all members have not the same office: so we, [being] many, are *one body* in Christ, and every one members one of another" (Ro 12:4–5). All of us who choose to be born again, belong to *the one body of Christ.* 1 Corinthians 12:12–14, 12:27 also says,

> For as *the body is one*, and hath many members, and all the members of that [one] body, being many, are one body: so also [is] Christ (in this manner, Christ also). For by *one spirit* are we all *baptized* into one body (spirit, not water), whether [we be] Jews or Gentiles, whether [we be] bond or free; and have been all made to drink [into] one Spirit (and all have been given to drink *one spirit*). For the body is not one member, but many. Now *ye are* [the] *body of Christ*, and members in particular."

Here we have baptism and spirit in the same verse. In this case, the word drink (*potizo*) means to irrigate, to give or furnish drink, as in a cup of cold water (Mt 10:42) or milk (1Co 3:2), or to "watereth" (1Co 3:7–8). It implies being refreshed by way of the gift of holy spirit.

Ephesians 4:4–6 goes on to say that "[There is] *one* body, and *one* spirit, even as ye are called in *one* hope of your calling; *one* Lord (Jesus Christ), *one* faith, *one* baptism, *one* God and Father of all, who is above all, and through all, and in you all." There are no twos or threes or fours; just ones.

These verses are the formula for unity in the Church of the Body of Christ. Ephesians is the greatest doctrinal epistle given to us. Here we have seven "ones"! Seven is the number of spiritual perfection.[4] Unity will never be achieved in the Christian Church, without rightly dividing these seven pinnacles of truth. We are many members, but one body, in Christ.

Romans 12:4 gives us a clue as to our function as members in the Body of Christ: "For as we have many *members* in one body, and all members have not the same office: so we, [being] many, are one body in Christ, and every one members one of another." Here, "office" is the word *praxis* (4234), which means practice or mode of acting; by extension, a function. You might say that we do not all have the same job to do, yet, whatever we do compliments everyone in the body. "Members" (*melos*, 3196), means a limb or part of the body; thus, we are all mutually attached to and dependent on one another, implying a sense of responsibility to each other.

---

4   Bullinger, *The Companion Bible*, appendix 10, page 14

The *Charismata*

> Having then gifts (*charisma, charismata*) differing (that
> vary in kind) according to the grace (*charis*) that is given
> to us, whether prophecy (*propheteia*), according to the
> proportion of faith (our believing); or ministry (*diakonia*,
> service), on serving; or he that teacheth (*didasko*, to hold
> dialogue with another in order to instruct), on teaching; or
> he that exhorteth (*parakaleo*, to comfort and encourage), on
> exhortation; he that giveth (*metadidomai*, sharing anything),
> with simplicity (*haplotes*, without dissimulation or self-
> seeking); he that ruleth (*proistemi*, to be over or before),
> with diligence (*spoude*, care-full-ness); he that sheweth mercy
> (*eleeo*, to be compassionate, helpful and kind to all), with
> cheerfulness (*hilarotes*, happy to do it). (Ro 12:6–8)

The word "gifts" is used to describe our possible functions. Gifts are a
subject that is very misunderstood in the churches. There are many different
Greek words used to describe different types of gifts. Here, in Romans
12:6, "gifts" is *charisma, charismata* (5486), as in "a gift of grace, a spiritual
endowment; (subjectively) religious qualification, or (objectively) miraculous
faculty."[5] *Charismata* comes from *charizomai* (NT:5483), "to grant as a favor
[...] in kindness, pardon or rescue." It is the middle voice of *charis* (khar'-
ece, NT:5485), "the divine influence upon the heart and its reflection in
life."

In the above passage, there is another list of seven—seven *charismata*
gifts—mentioned in one place. Each is a gift of God's favor and they are
developed over time. New Christians may not be as inclined to "showing
mercy" to one another, as they are to "giving." But, seasoned Christians
could excel in several of these gifts. One of the challenges is discovering
which of these gifts we may have. Are there any of these gifts to which you
feel particularly inclined? Are any of them something that you love to do,

---

[5]   See Strong's.

something you are good at doing? All *charismata* differ, yet they are all gifts of the grace of God.

There are more gifts and manifestations in 1 Corinthians 12, where we read,

> And God hath set (placed) some in the church, first apostles, secondarily prophets, thirdly teachers, after that miracles (*dunamis*, inherent power) then gifts of healings (*charismata* of *iama*, curing sicknesses) helps (*antilepsis*, providing aid or relief) governments (*kubernesis*, to steer, pilot or direct) diversities (*genos*, kinds) of tongues (*glossa*, languages). (28)

In this verse alone, there are three of the five "equipping ministries" mentioned in Ephesians 4:11, three of the nine manifestations of the spirit mentioned in 1 Corinthians 12:7–10, and two *charismata*. God has placed all these in the Church. But how many apostles, prophets, teachers, workers of miracles, or individuals operating gifts of healing do you know? And, *where* are they? Later in 1 Corinthians 12, we have seven questions: *the third set of sevens*. "[Are] all apostles? [are] all prophets? [are] all teachers? [are] all workers of miracles? Have all the gifts of healing? do all speak with tongues? do all interpret?" It is easy to assume that the answer to these questions is, "Absolutely not." What this version of the verse hides is an untranslated Greek word that begins each of these seven questions. The word is *Mee'*, which means "no" or "not,"[6] but not absolutely.[7] It does not mean that we cannot be or do any one of those things, at all. *Mee'* could be translated as "possibly" or even "maybe." Thus, these questions could just as easily be answered "yes," depending on the individual and the circumstances.

---

6   NT:3361 *me* (may); a primary particle *of qualified negation* (whereas NT:3756 expresses an *absolute denial*). Strong's

7   There are two principle negatives used in the New Testament: *ou* and *me. Ou* means no, not; expresses full and direct negation, independently and absolutely; not depending on any condition expressed or implied. *Me* also means no, not; expressing *conditional* negation, depending on *feeling*, or on some idea, conception, or hypothesis. Bullinger, *The Companion Bible*, appendix 105, page 150.

Knowledge is empowering, but true knowledge is even more empowering. These verses have been so perverted in the doctrine of the Church, that the things mentioned in them are no longer relevant. There is so much empowering ability, which is ours to claim in His Word, but if we do not know it or have been talked out of it, we cannot walk in the power that is ours. The Old Testament believers would roll over in their graves if they could see what we have, in the spirit. Very few of them had spirit upon them and, even then, it was conditional, meaning that if they messed up, the spirit departed; left them high and dry. We have the spirit of God sealed in us, unconditionally, so no matter what we do, it cannot be changed, altered, or corrupted.

> In whom ye also [trusted], after that ye heard the word of truth, the gospel of your salvation: in whom also *after that ye believed, ye were sealed* with that holy spirit of promise. (Eph 1:13)

> And grieve not the holy spirit of God, whereby ye are *sealed unto* [the] *day of redemption.* (Eph 4:30)

> Being born again, not of corruptible seed, but *of incorruptible*, by [the] word of God, [which] liveth and abideth (living and abiding) [for ever]. (1Pe 1:23)

The Gift of holy spirit is Sealed in Us

The free gift of holy spirit is the primary thing that sets us apart from Old Testament believers. We are spoiled with something that would be unimaginable to them. And, so, where are the apostles, the prophets? Have you ever heard speaking in tongues with interpretation in your church, for the edification of the members? Is anyone known for performing works of power or gifts of healings? Even though there are some who make an attempt to lead such lives, very few do. I doubt that more than 1 percent of worshippers in the church today worship in spirit and in truth. Most believers are still praying for God or Jesus to do what they have already done.

Before I continue outlining all the different kinds of gifts, I want to look at a few more general scriptures on the subject. In Romans 1:11 we read, "For I long to see you, that I may impart unto you some spiritual (*pneumatikos*)[8] gift (*charismata*) to the end ye may be established (*sterizo*)." The *charismata* gifts are considered *spiritual*; of or pertaining to the spirit; of or from God. Paul earnestly wanted to see the believers, so that he could give them a spiritual gift. He did so in order to insure that they may be established in the Word, set fast, made stable, or strengthened. One of the purposes of the *pneumatikos* is to prevent us from being blown about with every wind of doctrine (Eph 4:14). Established (*sterizo*) means to be turned resolutely, in a certain direction, not just any direction. What a lot of us fail to understand initially, is that Paul did the imparting, the giving over (Ro 1:11). Once we have these gifts, we can share them with others. A *charismata* is something we can give to one another on a horizontal plane.

In our culture, a gift is given to someone in order to bless that person. In some eastern cultures, like that of the Bible, a gift is given not only to bless the recipient, but also as an act of grace on behalf of the giver. The whole point behind receiving things from God is to freely give what you have received. 1 Peter 4:10 says, "As every man hath received [the] gift (*charismata*), [even so] *minister* [the] *same one to another*, as good stewards of the manifold grace of God." This is probably one of the most important aspects of stewardship: the spiritual giving of what we have received to others, to the end that they too become established. Matthew corroborates this truth in 10:8: "Heal the sick, cleanse the lepers, raise the dead, cast out devils: *freely ye have received, freely give*." In some Christian circles, it is commonplace to hear members ask one another if they would like to be "ministered to." If God did not make *ministering the charismata* of "healing, cleansing, raising and casting" one another available to us, we would not be told to do so. Ministering the *charismata* and the giving of grace are acts of unselfish love, as with the operation the manifestations of the spirit.

---

[8] NT:4152 *pneumatikos, pneumatikee, pneumatikon*: spiritual; belonging to the Divine Spirit; a. in reference to things; emanating from the Divine Spirit, or exhibiting its effects and so its character: charisma, Ro 1:11; b.in reference to persons; one who is filled with and governed by the spirit of God: 1 Co 2:15. Thayer's

The *Dorea* Gifts

In Acts 2:38, Peter said unto the Jews, "repent, and be baptized every one of you in the name of Jesus Christ for the remission of sins, and ye shall receive the gift *(dorea)*, of/from the Holy Spirit, who is God." This gift is a present from God; it is the gift of holy spirit. It is from this gift that all other gifts and manifestations spring. Without this one, no others are possible. To receive this gift you must be born again.

> And they of [the] circumcision which believed were astonished, as many as came with Peter, because [that] on the Gentiles also was poured out the *gift (dorea)*, from The Holy Spirit. For they heard them speak with tongues, and magnify God. (Ac 10:45–46)

Normally, those that received the gift of holy spirit spoke in languages they themselves did not know (speaking in tongues). As always, the words they spoke magnified God.[9]

> (But not as the offence, so also [is] the free gift *(charismata)*. For if [through] the offence of *one* ('Adam, man) many be dead much more the grace of God, and the gift *(dorea)* by grace, which by *one* man, Jesus Christ, hath abounded unto many. And not as [it was] by one that sinned, [so is] the gift *(dorea)*, for the judgment [was] by *one* to condemnation, but the free gift *(charismata)* [is] of many offences *unto justification*. For if by *one man's* offence death reigned by one; much more they which receive abundance of grace and of the gift *(dorea)*, of righteousness shall reign in life by *one, Jesus Christ*.[10]) (Ro 5:15–17)

---

9   NT:3170 *megalunoo*; 1. to make great, magnify Mt 23:5; 2. to deem or declare great, i. e., to esteem highly, to extol, to laud, to celebrate: Lk 1:16. Thayer's

10   Please note that these verses are parenthetical figures of speech, which started in verse 13.

This gift (*dorea*) was made available by the obedience unto death of the man, Jesus Christ, who remedied the offence of the first man, Adam. You can see here that justification and righteousness come with receiving the *dorea* type of gift. These verses also say that, as death *reigned* through Adam, so righteousness will *reign* through Jesus Christ. This is why Jesus Christ is called the last Adam, because he was the perfect sacrifice for our sin! 1 Corinthians 15:45–47 confirms this:

> And so it is written, The first man (*anthropos*), Adam was made a living soul; the last Adam [was made] a quickening[11] spirit. Howbeit, [that was] not first which is spiritual, but that which is natural; [and] afterward that which is spiritual. The first man [is] of [the] earth, earthy: the second man (*anthropos*), [is the Lord] from (out of) heaven

> Who verily was foreordained before the foundation of the world, but was manifest in these last times for you. (1Pe 1:20)

Ephesians also speaks of the *dorea* type of gifts:

> Whereof I was made *a minister* (*diakonos*, one who executes the commands of another, like Jesus Christ) according to the gift, *dorea* of the grace of God given unto me by the effectual working of his power. (3:7)

> But unto *every one of us* is given grace (*charis*), according to the measure of the gift (*dorea*) of Christ. (4:7)

No one who chooses to believe is missed!

Dorea predominantly refers to gifts that descend vertically down from God, who is the Holy Spirit, as in Acts 2:38. Or they emanate from Jesus Christ, as in Ephesians 4, when a person is saved by grace. On the other

---

[11] NT:2227 *zooopoieoo*; *zooopoioo*; 1. to produce alive, beget or bear living young; 2. to cause to live, make alive, give life: 1 Ti 6:18. Thayer's

hand, *charismata* refers to those gifts given to one after they have been born again of God's spirit, by making Jesus their Lord and believing that God raised him from the dead. The *charismata* are all-inclusive and can be ministered between one another.

The *Doma* Gifts

> Wherefore he saith, When he ascended up on high, he led captivity captive, [and] gave (giving, *gifts*, *doma*) unto men. And he gave some, apostles; and some, prophets; and some, evangelists; and some, pastors and teachers; For the perfecting (complete equipping) of the saints, for the work of the ministry, for the edifying of the body of Christ. (Eph 4:8, 4:11–12)

These five *doma* gifts are given to us by Jesus Christ himself. Verse 12, above, tells us the purposes for which they were given:

1. "for the perfecting (*katartismos*)," complete furnishing. *Katartismos* comes from *katartizo*: to equip, put in order, strengthen, to make us what we ought to be (1Co 1:10; 1Pe 5:10).
2. "for the work (*ergon*)," that which needs to be accomplished.
3. "for the edifying (*oikodome*), the act of building, building up (1Co 14:5, 14:12, and 14:26; Eph 2:21, 4:16, and 4:29).

Ephesians 4:13 tells us how long these gifts are in effect: "Until we all come in the unity of the faith (of Jesus Christ,) and of the knowledge of the Son of God, unto a perfect man, unto [the] measure of the stature of the fullness of Christ." Thus, they must still be in effect. Ephesians 4:14 tells us why these gifts are so important: "That [we henceforth be] no more children, tossed to and fro, and carried about with every wind of doctrine (*didaskalia*) by the sleight (fraud), of men, [and] (with) *cunning* craftiness, whereby they lie in wait to deceive (plan methodically to lead astray)." These words recall those of the apostle Peter: "For we have not followed *cunningly* devised fables" (2Pe 1:16). These cunningly devised myths or sophisms are designed to perpetrate "plausible, believable, error."[12]

The purpose of the *doma* gifts is to keep us out of the stew! The perpetrators of myth that Paul is talking about, are people inside, not outside, the Church. People outside the Church do not care what we think or believe. When 1 John speaks of antichrists, it means those who "went out from us."

All these "equipping gift ministries" need to be operative in our churches, not just in our pastors. It seems like everyone I meet in church today is a pastor. It is almost as if every believer is a pastor. I have even been called a pastor, but I am certainly not a pastor. I could be, if circumstances required it, but it is not my calling. My wife is a pastor, or what it really is to be a pastor: a shepherd. She cares for people, attends to their needs, and has intimate relationships with them, like a shepherd would their sheep. It is these traits that define a pastor's true calling.

These five ministries were given to the Church by Jesus Christ, who is its head. Paul speaks of such in regards to Jesus in Ephesians:

> And hath put all [things] under his feet, and gave him [to be the] *head* over all [things] to the church, which is his body, the fullness of him that filleth all in all. (1:22–23)

> But speaking the truth in love, may grow up into him [in] all things, *who is the head*, [even] Christ. (4:15)

> For [the] husband is [the] head of the wife, even as Christ [is the] head of the church: [and] he [is the] saviour of the body. (5:23)

Here, the word "head (*kephale*)" is derived from the root *kapto* and means to seize, in the sense that the head is readily taken hold of, literally or figuratively. This is to say that Christ sticks his neck out for us every

---

[12] See Chapter V, footnote 9 *Sophizo*; For "cunning craftiness," see Chapter V, footnote 16. This is the word *panourgia,* which is translated as "subtilty" in 2Co 11:3.

day. He goes to bat for us against our adversary, the Devil. Husbands are to do the same for their wives, like when a man walks closest to the street when walking with a woman down the sidewalk. In this context, being the "head" is not for the purpose of lording over, but for the purpose of giving your life, as Christ did for us.

The Manifestation of the Spirit

To conclude the subject of gifts, let us look at one of the most misunderstood and erroneously interpreted passages of scripture written "to" the church. By now, we have seen many instances of [translator added words] in the Bible verses at which we have looked. Awareness of these additions helps to explain the verse, but it can also lead to confusion. This is the case with 1 Corinthians 12:1: "Now concerning spiritual [gifts] brethren, I would not [have] you ignorant." Here, in the KJV, "gifts" has been added by the translators. Spiritual (*pneumatikos*) is anything and everything emanating from or pertaining to *the spirit*. Paul is saying that he does not want us to be ignorant of spiritual things. The verse should begin, "Now, concerning spiritual things brethren." The word ignorant (*agnoeo*, NT:50) has a two-fold meaning: not to know (through lack of information or intelligence); or, by implication, to ignore (through disinclination). Someone may be ignorant through a lack of information or by choosing to be disinclined to know, thereby ignoring the truth.

1 Corinthians 12:3 says, "Wherefore I give you to understand, that no man speaking by (with or in) [the] spirit of God calleth Jesus accursed: and [that] no man can say [that] Jesus [is the] lord, but by [the] holy spirit." Here it should be obvious that Paul is still talking about spiritual, not carnal things. The word "the" was erroneously added three times: once before "spirit of God," once before "Lord," and once before "Holy Ghost." Capitalizing these words would be correct if the articles were actually in the texts, but since they are not, the words should not be capitalized. Lower case "holy spirit" is the gift of upper case Holy Spirit and the two have ever been confused by that little three letter word, *the*.

This is something Paul really wants us to understand. Anyone can call out, "Jesus accursed" and anyone can say, "Jesus, Lord" with their mind or understanding. But, Paul is not talking about using your mind or your understanding to do it. He is talking about speaking or uttering words with the gift of holy spirit! This is exactly what happened on the day of Pentecost. This is speaking by, with, or in the spirit, not in the language(s) you know. We have all ready read records of this in the book of Acts.

In 1 Corinthians 12:4–6, the uncommon word *diaresis* (diversities, differences, distributions, distinctions, divisions) appears.[13] These verses are the only place in the Bible where the word is used:

> Now there are *diversities* of gifts, but the same Spirit. And there are *differences* of administrations,[14] but the same Lord. And there are *diversities* of operations,[15] but [it is] the same God which worketh all in all.

The *charismata* gifts are distributed on a large scale, as well as individually. Verse 5 above, speaks of different ways or classifications of serving, as discussed in Romans 12:7. In 1 Corinthians 12:6, there are distinctions between different *energema*, the effects of something wrought; the result of *energeia*. In classical Greek literature, these terms (including the verb *energeo*, to be at work) seem to have been used almost exclusively as medical terms, referring to medical treatment and the influence of medicine, which relates them to healing. So, in these verses from 1 Corinthians, we

---

[13] NT:1243 Dividing, distribution, classification or separation; Used in regard to gifts, services and results of energies or operations; from dia, 1223, involving separation and haireo, 138, to take grasp or sieze. Spiros Zodhiates, *Hebrew-Greek Keyword Study Bible.* (Chattanooga: AMG, 1991).

[14] NT:1248 *diakonia, diakonias, hee*; service, ministering; 1. universally: 2Ti 4:11; Heb 1:14; 2. of those who by the command of God proclaim and promote religion among men; a. of the office of Moses: 2 Co 3:7; b. of the office of the apostles and its administration: Ac 1:17,25; c. of the ministration or service of apostles, prophets, evangelists, elders, etc.: 1Co 12:5. Thayer's

[15] NT:1755 *energeema, energeetos, to*; thing wrought; effect, operation: 1 Co 12:6. Thayer's

have distributions of gifts, classifications of serving, and distinctions in spiritual energizings. Yet, grammatically, the most important word in verses 4–6 is the first word, "Now!" Like "but," "now" marks a change of structure in the chapter. Verses 1–3 tell us that speaking by the spirit of God, or holy spirit, is distinctly different than speaking as you know how to speak by nature. Verses 4–6 tell us the different ways that God and His Spirit work in the Church. Continuing on, verses 7–11 start with the word, "But," which is used to contrast what follows it with that which preceded it. Thus, these latter verses no longer concern gifts, the ways of serving, or the differences in the effects of something wrought. Instead, they speak of the "manifestation" of the spirit.

The word "manifestation" in 1 Corinthians 12:7, is *phanerosis*, which comes from the word *phaneroo* and means exhibition, to show proof of, to render apparent or make evident. It is used to make apparent or exhibit the different aspects of the gift of holy spirit. *Phanerosis* is only used twice in the Bible, but *phaneroo* (5319) is used 50 times. To gain a better understanding of what is meant by manifestation, let us look at a few of these instances:

> This beginning of miracles did Jesus in Cana of Galilee, and *manifested* forth his glory; and his disciples believed on him. (Jn 2:11)

The miracle that Jesus did was a *manifestation* of his glory. "Working of Miracles" is one of the manifestations recorded in 1 Corinthians 12:10.

> After these things Jesus *shewed* himself again to the disciples at the sea of Tiberias; and on this wise *shewed* he himself. (Jn 21:1)

Here, *phaneroo* is translated as "to show."

> Saying, What shall we do to these men? For that indeed a notable miracle hath been done by them [is] *manifest* to all them that dwell in Jerusalem; and we cannot deny [it]. (Ac 4:16)

Here, Peter operated the manifestation of miracles and healed a man. The healing was the undeniable proof, the manifestation of a miracle that occurred for all to *see* and to cause them to believe.

> For we must all *appear* before the judgment seat of Christ; that every one may receive the things done in his body, according to that he hath done, whether it be good or bad. Knowing therefore the terror of the Lord, we persuade men; but we are made *manifest* unto God; and I trust also are made *manifest* in your consciences. (2Co 5:10–11)

Here, the word is also translated as "to appear."

Besides Acts 2:4, there are two other clear records of the speaking in tongues being manifested by those who received the gift of holy spirit. Acts 10:45–46 says,

> And they of [the] circumcision which believed were astonished, as many as came with Peter, because [that] on the Gentiles also was poured out the *gift* (*dorea*) from The Holy Spirit. For *they heard them speak with tongues*, and magnify God.

The speaking in tongues was the evidence, the manifestation of the gift of holy spirit, which had been received. The reception of the gift was normally accompanied by speaking in languages the speakers themselves did not know.

This final account is particularly significant, because it shows that there was no manifestation of the spirit accompanying water baptism. Acts 19:2–6 says,

> He (Paul) said unto them, Have ye received [the] Holy Ghost (holy spirit) [since] ye believed? And they [said] unto him, We have not so much as heard whether there be [any] Holy Ghost (holy spirit). And he said [unto them], Unto what then were ye baptized? And they said, Unto John's baptism. Then said Paul, John [verily] baptized [with the] baptism of repentance, saying

unto the people, that they should believe on him which should come after him, that is, on [Christ] Jesus. When they heard [this], they were baptized in the name of the Lord Jesus. And when Paul had laid [his] hands upon them, [the] Holy Ghost (holy spirit) came on them; and they spake with tongues, and prophesied.

These believers not only spoke in tongues, but they also prophesied, which is another one of the manifestations of the spirit. These verses represent what happens when people are baptized with water and do not realize or know that God has so much more for them. Here, we see that the gift of holy spirit is *not* received with water baptism.

When we receive a gift of any kind from someone, we can usually see it, taste it, touch it, or smell it. We might get a new watch, pen, Bible, hammer, or shirt, but immediately we know what it is and its intended purpose. However, when we receive the gift of holy spirit, it is invisible and we cannot see it; we do not know if we really received anything and we have no proof of it. Without a "manifestation," you cannot know if you received anything! One cannot feel the true spirit of God. There is no biblical precedent for this. God wants us to know this. He made the manifestation of the Spirit available for that reason. Speaking in tongues and prophecy are only two of the manifestations of the spirit. There are nine manifestations or evidences of the indwelling spirit of the Almighty God, who created the Heavens and the Earth. God would not have us wondering.

1 Corinthians 12:7 says, "But the *manifestation* of the spirit is given to *every man* to profit [withal]." Since they have been given to everyone, no one misses out. No one can honestly say, "I haven't been given any of these supernatural abilities," unless they simply do not know it. Here, the word "to profit (*sumphero*)" means to bring together, to unify, to complete.[16] It comes from the primary preposition *sun*, which denotes

---

[16] *Sumphero* (soom-fer'-o); from NT:4862 and NT:5342 (including its alternate); to bear together (contribute), i.e. (literally) to collect, or (figuratively) to conduce;

union, and a primary verb *phero,* to bear or carry. Literally, it means to unify for the advantage or benefit of all. The word *hos* (3739) is used 1371 times in the New Testament, but only in this instance is it translated "to one." This alone should indicate that something is askew. The word for the numeral "one" is *heis* (1520). *Hos* is translated as this, that, who, which, whom, what, etc.; it is always neuter. It definitely does not mean "to one" particular person. In Matthew 11:4, *hos* is translated "those things which:" "Jesus answered [and] said unto them, Go [and] shew John again *those things which* ye do hear and see."

1 Corinthians 12:8–10 lists the nine different ways in which each of us can manifest the gift God has given to us. As with any list, something has to be first and something else has to be last. In the Bible, lists are not in order of priority, as some people wrongly teach. 1Corinthians 12:8–10 should read,

> For these are given by the Spirit: [the] word (or a message of) wisdom; another,[17] [the] word (or a message of) knowledge by the same Spirit; another, faith by the same Spirit; another, [the] gifts of healing by the one, *heis,* Spirit; another, [the] working of miracles; another, prophecy; another, discerning of spirits; another, [divers] kinds of tongues; another, [the] interpretation of tongues.

These nine ways are given to every believer by the one and selfsame Spirit, who is God. God accomplishes this through the spirit that He creates in you when you make Jesus your Lord and believe that God raised him from the dead.

Verse 11 goes on to establish that the ways to manifest the gift of God are given to everyone:

---

especially (neuter participle as a noun) advantage. Strong's

[17] NT:243 *allos, allee allo*; another, other; a. absolutely: Mt 27:42; b. as an adjective: Mt 2:12; c. with the article: *ho allos,* the other (of two), Mt 5:39 (Thayer's). You can see from the definition that there is no *"to."*

But, *all these* worketh (*energeo*, are energized by) that one (*heis*, 1520), and selfsame Spirit, dividing (*diaireo*, from *diaresis*; distributing) *to every man*, severally, their own (*idios*), as he will (*boulomai*, as each of us is so minded or willing).[18]

We have the freedom of will to operate all nine of these manifestations or none of them, but we can all operate all nine if we are willing.

In the passage above, "these," the word *tauta*, is in the neuter plural tense and refers to these nine things.[19] We also have the usage of *heis*, one. This should clearly demonstrate the difference between *heis* and *hos* and the mis-translation that occurred in the preceding three verses. We also see, for a second time, that *these* are given to every single believer, whether or not we have a desire to receive them or are so minded. We do not have the ability to manifest just one of these, but all of them!

These nine manifestations of the spirit are the evidence of the indwelling reality of God's primary, "free" gift to us. They are the proof that one really did receive the spirit from God when they believed. The nine manifestations of the spirit are part of the package deal we receive with the gift of holy spirit. We can operate each and every one of them in order to bring us closer together, as one body, in unity. They are for the edifying of the body of Christ! We do not have to ask for them, because we already have them. To manifest them, all we have to do is believe! More importantly, with the exception of the *charismata* of healing, which is still a manifestation, the rest are *not charismata* gifts. After reading this, no one can ever again say that they were not given the ability to speak in tongues, to interpret tongues, or to prophecy. Fear is the only thing that will keep you from it. This is one of the reasons that love is so important and why the greatest chapter in the Bible about the love of God is placed between two

---

[18] NT:1014 *boulomai*; to will, wish; 1. commonly, to will deliberately, to have a purpose, to be minded: followed by an infinitive, Mk 15:15; 2. Of willing as an affection, to desire: followed by an infinitive, 1Ti 6:9. Thayer's

[19] NT:5023 *tauta* (tow'-tah); nominative or accusative case neuter plural of NT:3778; these things. Strong's

chapters dedicated to the manifestations of the spirit. It takes the love of God to operate them. Paul tells us time and time again to love one another without dissimulation. We know from Jesus' teachings that we have to love ourselves in order to truly love one another. The manifestations of the spirit are given to us in order to edify ourselves, one another, and subsequently, the Church. They are of the spirit, not the flesh.

1 Corinthians 14:3–5 says that speaking in tongues with interpretation and prophecy edifies, exhorts, and comforts the Church. It is an act of love to stand before your congregation and bring forth inspired utterances that edify, exhort, and comfort those present. 1 Corinthians 13 does not say that the love of God is more important than the manifestations that it names in the first two verses. Rather, it instructs us to operate them with the love of God. Ask anyone who has given a message of prophecy before their congregation or to an individual; it takes love to do it. It is an act of kindness.

Since the original Word of God was not divided into chapters, let us read these verses as if they were not separated:

> But now faith, hope, love, abide these three; but [the] greatest of these [is] love. Pursue love, *yet* desire earnestly[20] spiritual (things), but especially that you may prophesy. For one who speaks in a tongue does not speak to men but *to God*; for no one understands, but *in his spirit* he speaks mysteries (divine secrets). But one who prophesies speaks to men for edification and exhortation and consolation. One who speaks in a tongue *edifies* himself; but one who prophesies *edifies* the church. NASU (1Co 13:13–14)

> Now *I wish that you all spoke in tongues*, but even more that you would prophesy; and greater is one who prophesies than one

---

[20] NT:2206 *zeelooo, zeeloo*; to burn with zeal; 1. absolutely, to be heated or to boil Ac 7:9, 17:5; 2. transitive, *ti*, to desire earnestly, pursue: 1Co 12:31, 14:1, 14:39; a. to desire one earnestly, to strive after, busy oneself about him: to exert oneself for one (that he may not be torn from me), 2Co 11:2; b. to envy one: Ge 26:14. Thayer's

who speaks in tongues, *unless he interprets*, so that the church may receive *edifying*." NASU (1Co 13:5)

Here, we are told to pursue, run after the love of God and to have a zealous passion for those things pertaining to the spirit, namely speaking in tongues, interpretation of tongues, and prophecy. These things not only build up the individual who operates them, but they build up the Church, as well. If you love God's people, the Church, you should want to do everything you possibly can to build it up.

The edification of the Church is a big deal to God. The Church is a spiritual body. God did not give us of His Spirit so that we could sit on it, so to speak. He gave it to us to use for our own edification and for that of the spiritual body of Christ. There can be no true edification outside of these parameters. Everything else is just blowing smoke. Receiving the gift of holy spirit was the promise of the Father, about which Jesus told his Disciples prior to his ascension. From the day of Pentecost through the book of Acts, practically every time the gift of holy spirit was received, the manifestation of speaking in tongues and/or prophesy accompanied it. On the occasions that it did not occur, ignorance of its availability was the reason why.

1 Corinthians 14:12–13 says, "Even so ye, forasmuch as you are zealous of spiritual things, *seek that you may excel to the edifying of the church.* Wherefore let him that speaketh in a tongue, pray that he may interpret" AT. Paul encourages us to strive to go over and above in edifying the Church, which is the Body of Christ, in our zealous operation of spiritual things, especially the manifestations. Here, he also tells us that those of us who speak in tongues need to pray or believe in order to interpret, so that the church may be edified. The person who speaks in tongues is the one who is charged with the interpretation of the tongue he speaks; he does not translate the message, he interprets it.[21]

I will close this section with the last few verses of 1 Corinthians 14:

---

[21] NT:1329 *diermeeneuoo*; to interpret, to unfold the meaning of what is said, explain, expound: Lk 24:27; Thayer's

> If any person who thinks himself to be a prophet, or *spiritual*, let him acknowledge that the things which I write unto you are *commandments* of the Lord. But if any one be ignorant, let him be ignorant. Wherefore, brethren, covet to prophesy, and forbid not to speak with tongues. Let all things be done decently and in order. (37–40)

It is fascinating that, here, the word "covet" is used in a positive sense. We have learned not to covet anything, but here, we are strongly encouraged to do so. "Covet (*zeloo*, 2206; see footnote 20, above)" is the same word used in 1 Corinthians 14:1, where we are told to earnestly desire (*pneumatikos*). Paul began the chapter and ended it with the same exhortation. Thus, this should not be taken lightly, at all. It does not seem to matter to the Church that these things are the commandments of our Lord, Jesus Christ. The promise of the Father, which Jesus died to secure for us, is largely being ignored. It is a shame to look back at all the faithful men and women who stood for God—many of them to their deaths—and to see how today's leaders are seemingly unappreciative of their sacrifices.

The Principle of Giving

The sharing of what you have is a biblical principle that not only blesses the recipient, but the giver as well. It has come to be known as "tithing." Abram was the first one in the Bible to give away a tenth "of the spoil" from a victory in battle, as is recorded in Genesis 14. Returning from battle, Abram was greeted by two kings, one bearing gifts of his own and the other, demands. Genesis 14:18 reads, "And Melchizedek king of Salem brought out bread and wine. (He was priest of God Most High.)" ESV. It is important to note that Melchizedek did not come empty handed; he actually initiated the blessing, as verse 19 says. Abram then chose to give him a tenth of the spoils. It was Abram's choice, because the other king wanted something as well. Abram chose not to give that king what he wanted. At this point in time, Abram was a Gentile and the nation of Israel was not yet.

As time went on, the practice of tithing was incorporated into the Law of Moses and was designated to support the Levites.

> For the tithe of the people of Israel, which they present as a contribution to the Lord, I have given to the Levites for an inheritance. Therefore I have said of them that they shall have no inheritance among the people of Israel. ESV (Nu 18:24)

The tithes were always represented as something to eat or drink, from trees, from the ground, or from animals. The passage of scripture most often quoted on this subject is from the book of Malachi:

> Bring ye all the tithes into the storehouse, that there may be *meat* in mine house, and prove me now herewith, saith the Lord of hosts, if I will not open you the windows of heaven, and pour you out a blessing, that [there shall] not [be] room enough [to receive it]. (Mal 3:10)

The key word is "meat," something to eat or drink. The word is never mentioned in the Church Epistles. The only place it is mentioned in the New Testament is in the book of Hebrews, which is written "to" the 12 Tribes of Israel. Hebrews 7:5 says, "And verily they [that are] of the sons of Levi, who receive the office of the priesthood, have a commandment *to take* tithes of the people *according to* the law." We know by now, that Jesus Christ fulfilled the Law and that we are no longer under the Law, but under Grace. The obligation, the expectation to give the tithe, was for Israel, not for the Church of the Body of Christ. Church leaders have no right or authority to expect or encourage anyone to give a tenth or any other percentages. When people who are regular "tithers," because they have been taught to do so as an obligation, do not or cannot tithe, they feel guilty and begin to condemn themselves, as if they were somehow sinning.

Ways of governing change with changes in administrations. The Christian Church did not exist when tithing was instituted as a law for

Israel. It only stands to reason that new guidelines would apply to this new creation, and there were. The principle of giving and receiving has replaced the obligation of the tithe. But, what did not change was the reciprocating purpose for which giving was instituted.

> For as touching *the ministering to the saints*, it is superfluous for me to write to you: For I know the forwardness of your mind (desire to give,) for which I boast of you to them of Macedonia, that Achaia was ready a year ago; and your zeal hath provoked very many. But this I say, He which soweth sparingly shall reap also sparingly; and he which soweth bountifully shall reap also bountifully. Every man according as he purposeth in his heart, [so let him give] *not grudgingly, or of necessity*: for God loveth a cheerful giver. And God is able to make all grace abound toward you; that ye, always having all sufficiency in all things, may abound to every good work. (2Co 9:1–2, 9:6–8)

The first thing to note in these verses is that one of the purposes of giving is to minister to the saints, not to maintain or build buildings, much like the tithe was for the needs of the Levites. Second, the analogy of sowing seed like a farmer is used: whether a lot or a little is sown or planted, the sower will reap accordingly. It does not say, "if you don't give at least this much, it won't do you any good." These verses go on to say that sowing (giving) is a matter of the heart, but should absolutely not be undertaken out of sorrow or a feeling of obligation. Indeed, it says that God loves a "cheerful" giver![22] We are to give hilariously! This is the only place in the Bible this word *hilaros* is used. If it hurts to give, you should not do it. There is no obligation to give anything to anyone, ever. But, it would be foolish not to. There is one thing that every one of us has the same amount of: time. You do not have to have money or possessions in order to give. What you do have to have, no matter what you give, is the right attitude.

---

[22] NT:2431 *hilaros* (hil-ar-os'); from the same as NT:2436; propitious or merry ("hilarious"), i.e. prompt or willing. Strong's

Now, brethren, we [wish to] make known to you the grace of God which has been given in the churches of Macedonia, that in a great ordeal of affliction their abundance of joy and their deep poverty overflowed in the wealth of their liberality. For I testify that according to [their] *ability,* and beyond [their] ability, [they gave] of their own accord (willingness,) begging us with much urging for the favor of participation in *the support of the saints,* and [this,] not as we had expected, but they first gave themselves to the Lord and to us by [the] will of God. So we urged Titus that as he had previously made a beginning, so he would also complete in you this gracious work as well. But just as you abound in every thing, in faith and utterance and knowledge and [in] all earnestness and in the love we inspired in you, see that you abound in this gracious work also. I am *not* speaking [this] as a command, but as proving through the earnestness of others the sincerity of your love also. For you know the grace of our Lord Jesus Christ, that though He was rich, yet for your sake He became poor, so that you through His poverty might become rich. I give [my] opinion in [this] matter, for this is to your advantage, who were the first to begin a year ago not only to do this, but also to desire [to do it.] But now finish doing it also, so that just as [there was] the readiness to desire it, so [there may be] also the completion of it *by your ability.* For if the readiness is present, it is acceptable according to what a person has, *not* according to what he does *not* have. For this is not for the ease of others and for your affliction, but by way of equality — at this present time your abundance being [a supply] for *their need,* so that their abundance also may become [a supply] for *your need,* that there may be equality; as it is written, HE WHO GATHERED MUCH DID NOT HAVE TOO MUCH, AND HE WHO GATHERED LITTLE HAD NO LACK.[23] NASU (2Co 8:1–15)

---

[23] This quotation comes from Exodus 16:18.

These are some wonderful verses on the subject of giving. Firstly, the Macedonians were not only *able*, but *willing* to give of themselves. No influences from outside of themselves made them willing to give. In order to help anyone with anything, these two ingredients must be present. If one is not willing, the ability to give does not matter. Secondly, again we have the support of our fellow believers, who are called the saints. It says that giving to one another in the household of God is to prove the sincerity of your love.[24] And finally, we can help supply the needs of other believers with our abundance, not from our lack thereof; not out of our own need. Someday, their abundance may supply our needs, as well.

Teachers of communism have used the preceding verses to support their false doctrine of equality. This would also be a good passage for the 99 percenters. But, it speaks not of the world, but about the Church and how it is supposed to function.

There is no biblical evidence that money was ever a part of tithing in the Old Testament and it does not specifically say that money played any role in giving in the New. But, it does not need to because it is a principle. You can give time, talent, money, food, clothing, shelter, mercy, grace, peace—just about anything—and reap whatever you sow. One may also sow anger, lawlessness, hatred, wrongfulness, rigidity, and even religiosity; they will reap their fruit as well. The important things to know is that you are free to give whatever you purpose in your heart to give and that you give with unburdened cheerfulness.

Some other key scriptures on this subject are Romans 12:13a: "Distributing[25] to the necessity of saints;" and Philippians 4:16, where the key word in the KJV is "communicate(d):"

---

[24] Gal 6:10: "As we have therefore opportunity, let us do good unto all men, especially unto them who are of *the household* of faith." Eph 2:19: "Now therefore ye are no more strangers and foreigners, but fellowcitizens with the saints, and of the *household of God*" KJV.

[25] NT:2841 *koinooneoo, koinoonoo*; a. to come into communion or fellowship, to become a sharer, be made a partner: Heb 2:14; b. to enter into fellowship, join oneself as an associate, make oneself a sharer or partner: 1 Ti 5:22. Thayer's

Notwithstanding ye have well done, [that] ye did *communicate*[26] with my affliction. Now ye Philippians know also, that in [the] beginning of the gospel, when I departed from Macedonia, no church *communicated* (2841) with me as *concerning giving and receiving*, but ye only. For even in Thessalonica ye sent once and again *unto my necessity*. Not because I desire a gift (*doma*): but I desire fruit that may abound to your account. (14–17)

It is written in the Scriptures: He (the man that feareth the Lord, that delighteth greatly in his commandments) gives freely to the poor. The things he does are right and will continue forever (Ps(s) 112:9). God is the One who gives seed to the farmer and bread for food. *He will give you* all the seed you need and make it grow so there will be a great harvest from your goodness. *He will make you* rich in every way so that you can *always* give freely. And your giving through us will cause many to give thanks to God. This service you do, not only helps the needs of God's people, it also brings many more thanks to God. *It is a proof of your faith.* Many people will praise God because you obey the Good News of Christ — the gospel you say you believe — and because you *freely share* with them and with all others. And when they pray, they will wish they could be with you because of *the great grace* that God has given you. Thanks be to God for his gift that is too wonderful for words. NCV (2Co 9:9–15)

"*He will make you* rich in every way so that you can *always* give freely." What a promise! We have already seen that giving is proof of the sincerity of our love for God, and now we see that it is also proof of our faith in God, to supply our need in abundant excess, above all we can ask or think! What it comes down to is how much we believe in God's ability to multiply the seed we sow. No one gets left out when we give of our abundance,

---

[26] NT:4790 *sungkoinooneoo*; to become a partaker together with others, or to have fellowship with a thing: with a dative of the thing, Eph 5:11. Thayer's

especially not the giver. The purpose of giving is to supply the needs of the saved, whether they are the ones teaching you the word or they are feeble. And of receiving, that fruit may abound to the account of the giver. When you give, you will receive a greater supply to give from. It has been said that you cannot out-give God. When we give with the right attitude, there is no limit to what God can supply.

It would be wonderful if the Church actually took into account the needs of the saints, especially the poorer ones, when it came to deciding where to spend the money it collects. The needs of the saints should come before those outside of the church. The poor who received those gifts in the Old and New Testaments were always the poor of Israel and those of the Body of Christ.

> If thou lend money to any of *my people* that is poor by thee, thou shalt not be to him as an usurer, neither shalt thou lay upon him usury (no interest). (Ex 22:25)

> But the seventh year thou shalt let it rest and lie still (the land;) that the poor *of thy people* may eat: and what they leave the beasts of the field shall eat. In like manner thou shalt deal with thy vineyard, and with thy oliveyard. (Ex 23:11)

> For the poor shall never cease out of the land: therefore I command thee, saying, Thou shalt open thine hand wide unto *thy* brother, to *thy* poor, and to *thy* needy, in thy land. (Dt 15:11)

> For it hath pleased them of Macedonia and Achaia to make a certain contribution for *the poor saints* which are at Jerusalem. (Ro 15:26)

The words "the poor" in 1 Corinthians 13:3 were added by the translators. The only other reference in the Epistles to *the poor* is in Galatians 2:10, where the other Apostles tell Paul and Barnabas to remember the poor, something they had already planned on doing.

There is no obligation to give anything to anyone. Some say the reason the Dead Sea is dead is because it has no outlet. There are many blessings available to us when we give of what we receive. Once we see and understand these, we will want to apply the principle of giving and receiving, cheerfully.

Characteristics of Paul's Leadership

> For yourselves, brethren, know our entrance in unto you, that it was not in vain: but [even] after that we had suffered before, and were shamefully entreated, as ye know, at Philippi, we were bold in our God to speak unto you the gospel of God with much contention. For our exhortation [was] not of deceit, nor of uncleanness, nor in guile: but as we were allowed of God to be put in trust with the gospel, even so we speak; not as pleasing men, but God, which trieth our hearts. For neither at any time used we flattering words, as ye know, nor a cloke of covetousness; God [is] witness: Nor of men sought [we] glory, neither of you, nor [yet] of others, when we might (or could) have been burdensome, as [the] apostles of Christ. But we were gentle among you, even as a nurse cherisheth her children: so being affectionately desirous of you, we were willing to have imparted unto you, not the gospel of God only, but also our own souls, because ye were dear unto us. For ye remember, brethren, our labour and travail: [for] labouring[27] (working in their trades) night and day, *because we would not be chargeable* (a financial burden), unto any of you, we preached unto you the gospel of God. Ye are witnesses, and God also, how holily and justly and unblameably we behaved ourselves among you that believe. (1Th 2:1–10)

---

[27] NT:2038 *ergazomai* (er-gad'-zom-ahee); middle voice from NT:2041; to toil (as a task, *occupation*, etc.), (by implication) effect, be engaged in or with, etc. Strong's

Here, there are a lot of great characteristics that all leaders should have, but the greatest of them all may be that Paul *worked for a living*, in addition to all the teaching and preaching he did. Even though Paul was considered a high-cast Jew, who was very well educated, he knew the trade of tentmaking. Paul did accept "communications" from the churches, but it was not because of something he desired personally, but that fruit would abound to them for giving. He did not depend on what churches gave to him and those who were with him. These verses emphasize that "we would not be chargeable[28] to anyone." Acts 18:1–3 tells us,

> After these things Paul departed from Athens, and came to Corinth; And found a certain Jew named Aquila, born in Pontus, lately come from Italy, with his wife Priscilla; (because that Claudius had commanded all Jews to depart from Rome:) and came unto them. And because he was of the same craft, he abode with them, and wrought (*ergazomai*): for by their occupation[29] they were *tentmakers*.

The apostle Paul chose to be as responsible as possible for his own needs, even though he and others like him had a right to receive "communications" from the Church. In the preceding verses, Paul said that he could have thrown his weight around as an apostle and been burdensome, but instead he chose to behave himself "holily, justly and unblameably!"

> Finally, brethren, pray for us, that the word of the Lord may have free course, and be glorified, even as [it is] with you: and that we may be delivered from unreasonable and wicked men: for all [men have] not the faith. But the Lord is faithful, who shall stablish you, and keep [you] from evil (in effect or

---

[28] NT:1912 *epibareo* (ep-ee-bar-eh'-o); from NT:1909 and NT:916; to be heavy upon, i.e. (pecuniarily) *to be expensive to*; figuratively, to be severe towards. Strong's

[29] NT:5078 *techne* (tekh'-nay); from the base of NT:5088; art (as productive), i.e. (specifically) *a trade*, or (generally) *skill*. Strong's

influence.) And we have confidence in [the] Lord touching you that ye both do and will do the things which *we command* [you.] And the Lord direct your hearts into the love of God, and into the patient waiting for Christ. Now *we command* you, brethren, in [the] name of our Lord Jesus Christ, [that] ye withdraw yourselves from every *brother* that walketh disorderly, *and not after the tradition which he received of us.* For yourselves know how [ye] ought to follow us: for we behaved not ourselves disorderly among you; neither did we eat any man's bread for nought; but wrought with labour and travail night and day, that we might not be chargeable to any of you: not because we have not power, but to make ourselves an ensample unto you to follow us. For even when we were with you, *this we commanded you*, that *if any would not work, neither should he eat.* For we hear [that there are] some which walk among you disorderly, working not at all, but are busybodies. Now them that are such *we command and exhort by* [our] *Lord Jesus Christ*, that with quietness they work, and eat their own bread (not mooching off everyone else.) But ye, brethren, be not weary in well doing. And if any man obey not our word by this epistle, note that man, and have no company with him, that he may be ashamed. Yet count him not as an enemy, but admonish him as a brother. (2 Th 3:1–15)

Here, we receive another commandment: to abstain from associating with any fellow believer who is insubordinate to the teachings transmitted by Paul. Specifically, Paul refers to those in the Church who do not work, as disorderly, three times. He states that this type of behavior is not in accordance with the example that he set. Again, Paul says that he and those who labored with him could have taken eating other people's food for granted, but chose to work night and day, so that they would not be chargeable to anyone. This is the example they set for other's to follow.

And a second commandment is given: that anyone who refused to work should not be allowed to eat! That is great motivation to work. Those whom

Paul refers to as busybodies, are those who mill around others who are working in order to give the appearance that they too are working. Then, there is a third commandment: that these disorderly busybodies work, without talking or milling around, and eat their own food, not everyone else's. If anyone should continue to be disobedient to the exhortations from this letter to the Thessalonians, they were to be denied company, in hopes that they would be ashamed and make a turn around. Lastly, Paul says not to count him as hostile, but to warn him as a brother. Carrying your own weight in the Church is a big deal to God and to Jesus Christ.

All of the Apostles had the right to be compensated to do what they did. Continuing in Acts 20:33–38, Paul says,

> I have coveted[30] no man's silver, or gold, or apparel. Ye yourselves know, that these (his own) hands have ministered unto my (his own) necessities, *and to them that were with me.* I have shewed you all things, how that so labouring ye ought to support the weak (feeble, powerless) and to remember the words of the Lord Jesus, how he said, It is more blessed to give than to receive. And when he had thus spoken, he kneeled down, and prayed with them all. And they all wept sore, and fell on Paul's neck, and kissed him, sorrowing most of all for the words which he spake, that they should see his face no more. And they accompanied him unto the ship.

Paul says that he coveted no one's silver, gold, or clothing. From the definition below, we can see he did not count on it, long for it, or lust after it. Paul showed them that, through working, they should support those in the Church who are incapable of working: the feeble. It is very difficult to support others when you are not working. Supporting others includes those who minister the Gospel.

---

[30] NT:1937 *epithumeo* (ep-ee-thoo-meh'-o); from NT:1909 and NT:2372; to set the heart upon, i.e. long for (rightfully or otherwise). Strong's

Let him that is taught [in] the word *communicate* (become a financial partner) unto *him that teacheth* in all good things. Be not deceived; God is not mocked: for whatsoever a man soweth, that shall he also reap. For he that soweth to his flesh shall of the flesh reap corruption; but he that *soweth to the spirit* shall of the Spirit reap life everlasting. And let us not be weary in well doing: for in due season we shall reap, [if] we faint not. As we have therefore opportunity, let us do good unto all [men], *especially* unto them who are of the household of faith. (Gal 6:6–10)

Am I not free? Am I not an apostle? Have I not seen Jesus our Lord? Are you not my work in [the] Lord? If to others I am not an apostle, at least I am to you; for you are the seal of my apostleship in [the] Lord. My defense to those who examine me is this: Do we not have *a right* to eat and drink? Do we not have *a right* (*exousia*, exercised power) to take along a believing wife, even as the rest of the apostles and the brothers of [the] Lord and Cephas? Or do only Barnabas and I not have *a right to refrain from working?* Who at any time serves as a soldier *at his own expense?* Who plants a vineyard and does not *eat the fruit* [of it?] Or who tends a flock and does not *use the milk* of the flock? I am not speaking these things according to human judgment, am I? Or does not the Law also say these things? For it is written in the Law of Moses, YOU SHALL NOT MUZZLE THE OX WHILE HE IS THRESHING. God is not concerned about oxen, is He? Or is He speaking altogether for our sake? Yes, for our sake (Church Leaders) it was written, because the plowman ought to plow *in hope*, and the thresher to thresh *in hope of sharing* the crops(s). If we sowed spiritual things (*pneumatikos*) in you, [is it] too much if we *reap* material things from you? If others share *the right* over you, do we not more? Nevertheless, we did not use *this right*, but we endure all things so that we will cause no hindrance to the gospel of Christ. Do you not know that those who perform sacred services eat the food of the temple, and those who attend regularly to the altar have their share from the altar? So also the Lord directed those who proclaim the gospel *to get their living from the gospel.* NASU (1Co 9:1–14)

Choosing to exercise the right to receive compensation is up to the individual. The ox, the plowman, and the thresher have the right to hope that they will be able *to share* the fruit of the work they do. It is not too much to ask that those who sow spiritual things, reap carnal things. Paul set an unparalleled example for us. After all, he had the right to refrain from working. Pastors today have the same right, but it is a good idea to have a plan B. There would not be any poor believers in any of the churches of this day and age, if pastors were operating within the guidelines of the Grace Administration, but they are not. The apostle Paul was an incredible example, in that he, for the most part, supported himself as a tentmaker (Ac 18:3).

Why did Paul write all of the Church Epistles and not Peter? Why did Jesus Christ choose Saul/Paul to give that revelation to? Even though Peter is thought of as the father of the Church, it was Paul who was chosen to preach the good news of Jesus Christ to foreigners and strangers—everyone who was not Jewish. Peter's ministry was specifically to Israel and the Jews. The word Peter (*petros*) means a piece of rock, while "rock (*petra*)" (Mt 16:18), denotes a mass of rock. Peter and Paul both helped build the church of the Body of Christ, though they were called to two separate groups of people. Today, the church is made up of more non-Jews than otherwise. Jesus knew that both men's hearts were for God, but obviously he saw something special in Paul's.

The Bride of Christ

The Church of the Body of Christ, to which every born-again believer belongs, is *not* the Bride of Christ. Christ was not a Christian, he was a Jew; one day he really will be King of the Jews. His bride is the faithful of Jacob (Israel), the Jews, as well as those who believed in YHWH prior to Israel and those sealed in the book of Revelation. He is their bridegroom. The word "bride (*numphe*, 3565)" is only translated as "bride" once in the

New Testament (in John). Five other times, it is translated as "daughter in law," and once as "daughter." In the book of Revelation, it is translated four times as "bride" and nothing in-between. The word "bridegroom (*numphios*, 3566)" is used 15 times in the Gospels and once in the book of Revelation. Both Revelation and the Gospels are thusly addressed to Israel, whose people had no knowledge of the Administration of the Sacred Secret. Nowhere in the Church Epistles are either of theses words used.

> He that hath *the bride* is bridegroom: but the friend of the bridegroom, which standeth and heareth him, rejoiceth greatly because of the bridegroom's voice: this my joy therefore is fulfilled. (Jn 3:29)

> And I saw the holy city, new Jerusalem, coming down from God out of heaven, prepared *as a bride* adorned for her husband. (Rev 21:2)

> Come hither, I will shew thee *the bride*, the Lamb's wife [...] and shewed me that city, the holy Jerusalem, descending out of heaven from God. (Rev 21:9–10)

> Had a wall great and high, *and* had twelve gates, and at the gates twelve angels, and names written thereon, which are of *the twelve tribes of the children of Israel.* (Rev 21:12)

These verses come after the Millennial Kingdom, in the final and Everlasting Kingdom of the New Heaven and New Earth.

The word "bridegroom" also only occurs in the Gospels and the book of Revelation, scriptures not specifically addressed to the Church of the Body. The first occurrence is in Matthew 9:15, where it says, "And Jesus said unto them, Can the children of the bridechamber mourn, as long as *the bridegroom* is with them? but [the] days will come, when ***the bridegroom*** shall be lifted away from them, and then shall they fast." These verses refer to Jesus as the bridegroom. He, the bridegroom, was lifted away, taken from them the day he ascended into heaven. The children of the bridechamber can only refer to Israel. Matthew 15:24 says, "But he answered and said, I am not sent but unto the lost sheep of the house of Israel." Jesus' mission was solely to Israel. The bride and the children of the bridechamber can only be the faithful of Israel. No one was born again back then; it was not possible. Those who are referred to as the church of the bride are not those who are born again of the spirit of God. No one in the Gospels or prior to them was born again, nor was anyone in the book of Revelation.

The mere fact that these words do not appear between the end of the gospel of John and the beginning of the book of Revelation, should be proof enough to even the unlearned, that the Church of the Bride of Christ is not the Church of the Body of Christ.

verse 1), formless and empty, but it had become that way. However they are translated, these words linguistically denote something gone wrong, laid waste, or judged. In the only other places in the scriptures where these terms are thusly combined alike, they refer explicitly to a desperate state of being that results from God's judgment.[6] Also, look again at Isaiah 14:16–17: "Is this the man that made the earth to tremble, that did shake kingdoms; That made the world (earth)[7] *as a wilderness,* and destroyed the cities thereof."

Let us look more closely at some easily read-over words: "and *darkness was* upon the face of the *deep* and the Spirit of God moved upon the face of the *waters*" (Ge 1:2). Sometimes we have to look at what a particular passage does not say, as well as what it does say. What the aforementioned verse does not say, is that God created the "darkness, the deep, and the waters." It only says that they were there, which begs the question: where did they come from? Or, from whom did they come and when? We all know what darkness represents, but biblically the word *chosek* means misery, destruction, death, and wickedness. "The deep *(tehowm)*" means an abyss; a raging mass of water. And "waters *(mayim)*" denotes wasted water: by euphemism, urine or semen. Does this sound like anything God would create?

In Genesis 1:11, God said, "*dasha' 'erets dasha' deshe,*" which means "bring forth the earth to sprout tender grass or herb." Evidently, the seeds of the earth and green grasses, as well as the seeds of fruit trees, must have already been there. Then, in Genesis 1:12, the earth did as God said. What we see from Genesis 1:2 on, is the restoration of an earth that was previously created in verse 1:1! The war in heaven between Michael and Lucifer wrought cataclysmic consequences upon the earth between Genesis 1:1–2. This helps to explain what happened to the dinosaurs and Neanderthal man, which no one can explain in any other way. It also lends support to carbon dating, so

---

[6] See Jer 4:23 and Isa 34:11.
[7] OT:8398 *tebel* (tay-bale'); from OT:2986; *the earth* (as moist and therefore inhabited); by extension, the globe; by implication, its inhabitants; specifically, a part. Land. Strong's

that Christians no longer have to find ways to discredit scientists, who have determined the age of certain fossils to be way beyond the age of *Adam.*

There are other names synonymous with Lucifer, which are used during and after he was cast down onto the earth: the great dragon (OT 8577, serpent; NT 1404, a fabulous kind of serpent that fascinates). The first usage of the word "serpent" is in Genesis 3:1 and the root meaning of the word is, "to hiss, mutter, whisper as do enchanters, with the element of fascination."[8] One thing to remember here, is that Lucifer did not lose any of his remarkable attributes when he was "cast down." He was still perfect in beauty and wiser than Daniel. The allied Chaldean word means, "to be bright" (Bullinger). Correspondingly, 2 Corinthians 11:14 says, "And no marvel: for Satan himself is transformed into an angel of light."

The Figure of Speech, *Hypocatastasis*

"Old (*archaios*)" denotes that which has been from the beginning; original, ancient. A "Serpent (*Ophis*, NT:3789)" is an artful, malicious person; sly and cunning. *Ophis* comes from the word *optanomai*, to gaze with eyes wide open, as at something remarkable. Anointed cherubs (cherubim) are similar to celestial or spirit beings. The Devil (*diabolos*, NT:1228), on the other hand, is prone to slander, a false accuser, a calumniator, a persecutor of good men, who estranges mankind from God and afflicts men with diseases, by means of demons who, by his bidding, take possession of them. He is the malignant enemy of God and His son, Jesus Christ. Satan (*satanas*) is a superhuman adversary; the great opposer; the prince of devil spirits.

> When Satan is spoken of as a "serpent," it is the Figure of Speech *Hypocatastasis* = Implication; it no more means a "snake" than it does when Dan is so called in Ge 49:17; or an animal when Nero is called a "lion" in 2 Ti 4:17 or when Herod is called a "fox" in Luke 13:32. It is the same figure when "doctrine" is called "leaven" in Mt 16:6. It shows that something much more real and truer to truth is intended.

---

[8] Strong's OT:5172.

All the confusion of thought and conflicting exegesis have arisen from taking literally what is expressed by Figures, or from taking figuratively what is literal. A Figure of speech is never used except for the purpose of calling attention to, emphasizing, and intensifying the reality of the literal sense and the truth of the historical facts.

We cannot conceive Eve as holding a conversation with a snake, but we can understand her being fascinated by one apparently 'an angel of light' (i.e. a glorious angel) possessing superior and supernatural knowledge.[9]

Adam and Eve were not deceived by a talking snake, they were deceived by the wisest, most cunning, and beautiful being God ever created. They were tricked into questioning and doubting what God had told them. All Satan did was add a word and leave out a word, thereby getting Adam and Eve to question. One word can make the difference between the truth and a lie. Are there any who are more prepared than they were?

The fall of Lucifer should serve as a great example to all of us. The Devil—Satan—had everything going for him: riches, honor, wisdom, beauty, and the ability to transform himself into a glorious, perfectly created angel of light and, eventually, one full of haughtiness and arrogance. His mission is deception; deceiving the world. And, he is doing an incredible job. He and his army of devil spirits, one third of the former angels of heaven (at least 36,000), know their end and they are hell-bent on taking as many as possible with them. John 10:10a refers to Satan as "the thief": "The thief cometh not but for to steal, and to kill, and to destroy." It is he who holds the power of death, not God. Hebrews 2:14 confirms this: "that through death, he (Jesus Christ) might destroy him who holds the power of death, that is, the devil." God is not responsible for people's deaths. Not a Sunday goes by without some minister standing in the pulpit crediting the "mysterious ways of God" for

---

[9]   Both quotations are from Bullinger, The Companion Bible, appendix 19.

something that Satan has done! Satan has practically destroyed the Church of this day and age with his lies.

In John 8:44, Jesus addresses the religious leaders of his time:

> Ye are of your father the devil, and the lusts of your father ye will do. He was a murderer from the beginning, and abode not in the truth, because there is no truth in him. When he speaketh a lie, he speaketh of his own: for he is a liar, and the father of it.

People are constantly pondering the question "WWJD? (What would Jesus do?)," as if he never got in anyone's face. Here, Jesus told the men that their father was the Devil. No one can have a father without seed. What we are seeing here is the unforgivable sin.

> Wherefore I say unto you, All manner of sin and blasphemy shall be forgiven unto men: but the blasphemy [against] the [Holy] Ghost (Spirit) shall not be forgiven [unto men]. And whosoever speaketh a word against the Son of man, it shall be forgiven him: but whosoever speaketh against the Holy Ghost, it shall not be forgiven him, neither in this world, neither in the [world] to come. (Mt 12:31–32)

If blasphemy against the Son of man is forgivable, but blasphemy against the Holy Spirit is not, then the Holy Spirit cannot be anyone or anything other than God Almighty. The men that Jesus was talking to were born of the seed of their father, the Devil: the unforgivable sin.

Satan's primary target is the body of people who are supposed to represent the One, True God; those who are supposed to represent the truth to the world. He has managed to deceive many with his lies. The Church is guilty of so much error it is pitiful. What I have pointed out thus far from the scriptures is contradictory to what most Christians believe. Satan's first big lie was, "Ye shall not surely die" (Ge 3:4). It is the same lie that preachers preach from the pulpit today! They say, "You don't die when you die; you go to live with the Lord or you go to hell to be tormented night and day," neither one of which is true.

When Satan deceived Eve, Adam went right along with her and transferred the dominion of the world, which God gave to him, to Satan. The dominion that God gave to Adam and Eve is described as *radah* (OT:7287): "to rule, to have dominion, to dominate, to tread down, to subjugate."[10] In Luke 4:6, when the Devil was tempting Jesus (only the Devil can tempt with evil, see Jas 1:13), it says, "And the devil said unto him, All this *power* will I give thee, and the *glory* of them: for that is delivered (surrendered, given into the hands of another) unto me; and to whomsoever I will I give it." Adam gave it to Satan.

The Prince of this World

In John 12:31, Jesus calls the Devil the "Prince of this world": "Now is judgment of this world: now shall the prince of this world be cast out." Here, Prince (*archon*) means first in rank or power; commander in chief. In Ephesians 2:2, the apostle Paul refers to him as "the Prince of the power of the air, the spirit that worketh in the children of disobedience." Power (*exousia*, 1849) herein denotes the power of choice; the liberty of doing as one pleases; physical and mental power; the power of authority (influence) and right; the power of rule and government. And, in 2 Corinthians 4:4, Jesus calls the Devil "the god (*theos*, the supreme authority) of this world (*aion*, age, perpetuity of time, forever and ever, until Rev 20:10)."

Yet, despite all this proof, preachers continue to say, "God is in control." It is true that *a god* is in control of the world, but not the One True God. The sad thing is that some preachers hate talking about the Devil because they think it gives him power, thus glorifying him. But, Satan already has the power and the glory, or else he could not have offered it to Jesus. All our preachers need to do is expose the Devil; shine some light on him so that people can see who he really is; that he is responsible for all of the calamity in the world today. Preachers give Satan power by saying, "God is in control." In attempting not

---

[10] Brown-Driver-Briggs Lexicon (Abridged)

to, they glorify him without even realizing it! And he is laughing his "tail" off because of it.

In the time before Jesus Christ's ministry, very little was known about the true nature of Satan, and thus, Yahweh was erroneously credited for everything. Jesus revealed the true identity of Satan as never before. For the first time, he took the blinders off the people, so that they could see the Devil for who he is. Jesus did not mince any words to the religious leaders either, saying that the Devil was their father, because they, in their ignorance (ignoring truth), did more to follow him than God the Father. Matthew 22:29 says, "Jesus answered and said unto them, Ye do err, not knowing the scriptures, nor the power of God." Failure to understand the scriptures and rightly divide them has thusly led to the proclaiming of much false teaching.

One of the reasons that the Church, as a whole, believes Yahweh is in control, is because its proponents do not understand the word "reign," which is the subject of so many popular Christian songs. In this context, the first usage of the word appears in Exodus 15:18: "The LORD shall reign for ever and ever." Here, "reign" does not mean rule. "Reign (*malak* (maw-lak'), OT:4427)" is "a primitive root; to reign; inceptively, to ascend the throne; causatively, to induct into royalty; hence (by implication) to take counsel."[11]

In the next usage of the word, "reign" is an entirely different word, which does mean to rule over: *radah* (OT:7287), "to rule, to have dominion, to dominate, to tread down, to subjugate; to scrape out."[12] Leviticus 26:17 says, "And I will set my face against you, and ye shall be slain before your enemies: they that hate you shall *reign* (*radah*) over you; and ye shall flee when none pursueth you." Yet another word for "reign" also means to rule: *mashal* (OT:4910), "to rule, to have dominion, to reign." Deuteronomy 15:6 says, "For the LORD thy God blesseth thee, as he promised thee: and thou shalt lend unto many nations, but thou shalt not borrow; and thou shalt *reign* over many nations, but they shall not reign over thee."

When it comes to dominion over the earth, the world, or us, "reign" is never used of the Father, Yahweh. In fact, in the first usage of *radah* in Genesis

---

[11] See Strong's.
[12] Brown-Driver-Briggs Lexicon (Abridged)

1:26, God is giving man dominion "over all the earth." God is not reigning, as in ruling over or dominating the earth and the inhabitants thereof; Satan is.

What do you see when you look around, the nature of God or that of Satan? The world and the inhabitants thereof, reflect the nature of he who is ruling. The only logical explanation that can be given as to why so many believers believe that God is in control, is centuries of wrong teaching and doctrinal error. It is the result of the blind leading the blind. 2 Corinthians 4:1–4 talks about this:

> Therefore [seeing] we have this ministry, as we have received mercy, we faint not; But have renounced the hidden things of dishonesty, not walking in craftiness, nor handling the word of God deceitfully; but by manifestation of the truth commending ourselves to every man's conscience in the sight of God. But if *our* gospel be hid, it is hid to them that are lost: In whom the god (*theos*) of this world (*aion*)[13] hath blinded (figuratively, obscured) the minds (*noema*, perception) of them which believe not, lest the light of the glorious *gospel of Christ*, which is [the] image of God, should shine [unto them].

Here, Paul is again speaking about his Gospel as the Gospel of Christ; the Gospel that is the express representation of God (*theos*). Has Satan successfully concealed this truth? Have we been blinded to Paul's Gospel? The truth of Paul's Gospel has been hidden from believers, as well as unbelievers; they too have been blinded. In the above passage, verse 2 speaks about the hidden things of dishonesty, walking in craftiness, and handling the Word of God

---

[13] NT:165 *aioon, aioonos, ho*; In Greek authors: A. age; B. an unbroken age, perpetuity of time, eternity; Hence, in the N.T. Used: 1. forever; a. universally: forever, John 6:51,58; with a negation: never, John 4:14; b. in hyperbolic and popular usage: from the most ancient time down (within the memory of man), from of old, Luke 1:70; 2. the worlds, the universe, i.e. the aggregate of things contained in time; 3. this age Mt 13:22; the future age Luke 20:35; i. e., the age after the return of Christ in majesty, the period of the consummate establishment of the divine kingdom and all its blessings. Thayer's

deceitfully. Paul is talking about those of us in ministry; not natural men. Let us look at these deliberate acts in more detail:

1. hidden things—concealed, secret.
2. of dishonesty—shameful, disgraceful; hence, concealed acts that produce shame in you and others by contact with them.
3. Craftiness—engaging others in superficially plausible, but fallacious methods of reasoning. They look and sound good on the surface, but are actually unsound and misleading.
4. handling deceitfully—adulterating the Word of God for the purpose of ensnaring, entrapping, and deluding.

Ephesians 4:14 encourages us further along these lines: "That [we henceforth be] no more children, tossed to and fro, and carried about with every wind of doctrine, by the sleight of men [and] cunning craftiness, whereby they lie in wait to deceive."

1. slight—figuratively, pretense, fraud which is cunning craftiness.
2. lie in wait—methodically plan.
3. deceive—to lead astray, away from the truth, as an impostor would.

If we have not renounced these things, we need to, "but by manifestation, exhibition, of the truth, commending, proving, ourselves to every man's conscience, what is morally good or bad, in the sight of God" (2Co 4:2b). A lot of believers like to quote Proverbs 27:17: "Iron sharpeneth iron; so a man sharpeneth the countenance of his friend." This verse somewhat parallels the previous one. We need to commend, prove, and demonstrate ourselves to each other's consciences in the sight of God. Most believers isolate themselves from anyone who does not think and believe what they do, so there is no "iron sharpening iron." To sharpen is to make keen; to be alert. We need to put ourselves in awkward, uncomfortable situations with other believers, so that we may dialogue with them. I do this often and receive a defensive first reaction. People say to me, "I don't want to argue about this," or "You're being critical." Sometimes they allow me to explain why dialogue is important for fellow believers. Once I do, many of my interlocutors do an about face; but many do not.

In Acts 17:2 it says, "And Paul, as his manner was, went in unto them, and three sabbath days *reasoned*[14] with them out of the scriptures." Paul spent three days with Jews, both men and women, in essence trying to persuade them of things concerning Christ. Many believed; some did not. When he went to Corinth he did the same thing. Acts 18:4 says, "And he reasoned in the synagogue every Sabbath, and *persuaded*[15] the Jews and the Greeks." He did the same thing again in Ephesus. We have to get over the fear of having heated discussions with each other and with unbelievers. If we are not willing to argue with one another, whereby we can make one another keener, we are not going to stand much of a chance persuading convicted unbelievers. This is another area where the Devil has won a great victory, because we view people who enjoy reasoning out of the scriptures as divisive troublemakers.

---

[14] NT:1256 *dialegomai* (dee-al-eg'-om-ahee); middle voice from NT:1223 and NT:3004; to say thoroughly, i.e. *discuss (in argument or exhortation).* Strong's
[15] NT:3982 *peitho* (pi'-tho); a primary verb; *to convince (by argument,* true or false); by analogy, to pacify or conciliate (by other fair means); reflexively or passively, to assent (to evidence or authority), to rely (by inward certainty). Strong's

CHAPTER VIII

GOING TO SLEEP

Sleep, the Grave, Hell and the Pit

In many instances, God refers to death and dying as sleep, sleeping, and even being asleep. In Deuteronomy 31:16, "the LORD said unto Moses, Behold, thou shalt *sleep* with thy fathers." He told the prophet Nathan to say the same thing to David in 2 Samuel 7:12: "And when thy days be fulfilled, and thou shalt *sleep* with thy fathers." In Psalms 13:3, David asked God, "lighten mine eyes lest I *sleep* the sleep of death." In speaking about Babylon, Jeremiah says, "sleep a perpetual sleep and not wake" (Jer 51:39). Acts 13:36 says, "David fell on sleep and was laid unto his fathers and saw corruption (rotted away)." In 1 Corinthians 11:30, Paul says, "For this cause many are weak and sickly among you and many sleep." 1 Thessalonians 4:14 says, "For if we believe that Jesus died and rose again, even so them also which sleep in Jesus will God bring with him." Verse 15 continues, "we which are alive and remain (at the Rapture of the Church) shall not precede them that are asleep," and verse 16 goes on to say, "the dead (those asleep) in Christ shall rise first."

Not only does the Word say that David slept with his fathers, it also says that he saw corruption, which means his body, deteriorated to dust. This is distinct from the Lord Jesus Christ, who was dead and buried three full days and three full nights, but whose body did not see corruption (rot away). Since King David is asleep in the grave with his father and all the fathers before him, including Moses, where do we come off thinking that, when we die, we go to be with Jesus?

In John 11:11, Jesus said to his Disciples, "Our friend Lazarus sleepeth; but I go, that I may awake him out of sleep." Two days earlier, Martha had sent a messenger to Jesus to tell him that her brother was sick, thinking he would come to Lazarus right away; but he did not. After two days, Jesus left to wake Lazarus. The Disciples thought that Lazarus really was sleeping, so Jesus "told them plainly, Lazarus is dead (*apothnesko*)" (Jn 11:14). When Jesus got there, Lazarus had been "in the grave four days already" (Jn 11:39). What is important here is that Jesus always did the Father's will (sickness and disease are never the Father's will). Up to this point, Jesus had raised a young girl who had just died, a young man who was on the way to be buried, and now, he was about to raise a friend that he personally loved, who had been dead at least 4 days, and whose body had begun to rot and stink.

We must look to John 11:4 to understand why God had Jesus wait: "This sickness is (*esti*, exists) not unto (*pros*, toward the purpose of) death, but for the glory of God, that the Son of God might be glorified thereby." *Esti* is the third person present indicative of *eimi*, to exist.[1] *Pros* (NT:4314) is a preposition of direction: forward to, towards; with the accusative it means to, toward; of the issue or end to which anything tends or leads.[2] God has no place in sickness or in death. Later, Jesus addressed Martha, "Said I not unto thee, that, if thou wouldest believe (*pisteuo*), thou shouldest see the glory of God?" (Jn 11:40). Then Jesus prayed, which is something he rarely, if ever, did before healing someone, for the sake of the people standing nearby:

> And Jesus lifted up [his] eyes, and said, Father, I thank thee that thou hast heard me. And I know that thou hearest me always: but because of the people which stand by I said [it,]

---

[1]   NT:2076, 1510, Strong's

[2]   Strong's

that they may believe (*pisteuo*) that thou hast sent (*apostello*)
me. (Jn 11:41–42)

Here, Jesus manifested the glory of God; and so can we.

In Matthew 9:24, Jesus said, "for the maid is not dead (*apothnesko*), but sleepeth." When he said this, the people in the house "laughed him to scorn." Her father believed that she was dead (*teleutao*), but also believed that if Jesus were to touch her, she would live. Jesus and the woman's father used two different words to describe the situation. This is an example of something that I have always stressed in my teachings: mindset. Most people would choose the mindset of the father, for fear of being laughed to scorn. This is why Jesus said, "Give place (*anachoreo*)," when he entered the house, which means leave, withdraw, return, or go back. Jesus instructed them to leave the house because of their unbelief, which they displayed by deriding him. When the people were "put forth (*ekballo*, ejected, driven out)," Jesus went into the room where the man's daughter was. "He went in, took her by the hand and she arose (*egeiro*, awakened)" (Mk 9:25).[3]

> And at that time shall Michael stand up, the great prince which standeth for the children of thy people (Israel): and there shall be a time of trouble (the Great Tribulation), such as never was since there was a nation *even* to that same time: and at that time (the end of the Great Tribulation) thy people (Israel) shall be delivered, every one that shall be found written in *the book* and many of them that *sleep* in the dust of the earth shall *awake*, some to everlasting life, and some to shame [and] everlasting contempt. (Da 12:1–2)

Here, again, we see that the dead are called "asleep," and the opposite of being asleep is being awake!

---

[3] For other accounts of this story, see Mk 5:22–42 and Lk 8:49.

98

Wherefore he saith, Awake thou that sleepest, and arise from
the dead, and Christ shall give thee light. (Eph 5:14)

Isaiah 26:19 says, "Thy dead men shall live, my dead body shall they
arise (*quwm*). Awake (*quwts*) and sing, ye that *abide* in dust: for thy dew
is as the dew of herbs, and the earth shall cast out the dead." Isaiah says,
"Wake up!" Death is such a harsh reality that it is no wonder that God
chose to use the word "sleep" to describe it, knowing that someday everyone
who had ever died would wake up. As it says in Genesis 3:19, "In the sweat
of thy face shalt thou eat bread, till thou *return* unto the ground; for out
of it wast thou taken: for dust thou art, and unto dust shalt thou return."
No one can return to somewhere they have never been. At death, one can
only return to where one has already been. No one *returns* to heaven or
paradise when they die, because they have never been there before! Unto
dust will the dead return and nowhere else.

Let us look at what else the Bible has to say about death. Psalms 6:5
says, "For in death there is no remembrance of thee: in the grave (*Sheol*)[4]
who shall give thanks?" In death, there is no memory or recollection of
anything and the dead are no longer able to give thanks or praise. Psalms
49:14–15 says,

> Like sheep they are laid in the grave (*Sheol*); death shall feed
> on them (gross); and the upright shall have dominion over
> them in the morning; and their beauty *shall* consume (decay)
> in the grave (*Sheol*), their dwelling (residence). But God will
> redeem (in the future at the Resurrection of the Just, the First
> Resurrection, see Rev 20:5–6) my soul from the power of the
> grave (*Sheol*): for he shall receive me. Selah.

---

[4] OT:7585 *she'owl* (sheh-ole'); or *sheol* (sheh-ole'); from OT:7592; Hades or the
world of the dead (as if a subterranean retreat), including its accessories and
inmates: KJV - grave, hell, pit. Strong's

Speaking of the raising of Jesus, Psalms 30:3 says, "O Lord, you brought up my soul from *Sheol*, restored me to life from among those gone down to the Pit." Verse 9 of the same chapter goes on to say, "What profit is there in my death, if I go down to the Pit? Will the dust praise you? Will it tell of your faithfulness?" No, it will not.

> For the living know they shall die: but the dead know not anything!, neither have they any more a reward (hire, wages;) for the memory of them is forgotten. (We have not forgotten them, they have forgotten us.) Also their love, and their hatred, and their envy is now perished; neither have they any more a portion (share) forever in anything that is done under the sun. (Ecc. 9:5–6)

> Whatsoever thy hand findeth to do, do with thy might, for *there is* no work (labor), nor device (reasoning or reckoning), nor knowledge (understanding), nor wisdom (skill) in the grave (*Sheol*, Hades, Hell, or Pit) whither thou goest. (Ecc. 9:10)

Here, not only do we see all the "attributes" of death, but we also see how *Sheol* is translated in the KJV, as grave, Hell, and the Pit. In reality, everyone who has ever lived and died, believer or not, goes to *Sheol*, which the Bible also calls Hades. Hebrews 9:27 says, "And it is appointed unto men once to die, but after this the judgment." With the exception of Jesus Christ, everyone who has died is still dead and still in the grave. The dead will remain in the grave until one of the Judgments or the Rapture of the Church. This verse tells us that, until there is a judgment, everyone is dead. And the dead do not even know it!

In 1 Corinthians 15:26, the apostle Paul wrote, by revelation from Jesus Christ, "The last enemy that shall be destroyed is death." Death is and always will be an enemy, until it is destroyed. Death is not the immediate doorway to a new life with God, Christ, and the Angels in Heaven or Paradise. If that were the case, death could hardly be viewed as an enemy.

Are people still dying? This is a good indication that death has not yet been destroyed.

If this is so, what about Enoch? Was he not translated? Where on earth did the translators come up with "translated" as a description of this action? "Translated (*metatitheemi*)" means to transfer, to change, or to transpose. Basically, God took Enoch from one place and put him in another, where he did not know anyone. God did so because Enoch's life and testimony was "that he pleased God," and he did not want to experience the death of anyone he knew.[5]

These revelations fly in the face of practically everyone, especially those who call themselves Christians. If "the dead" were somehow happy and alive now, in Heaven, the whole Bible would fall apart. No one is any good to God dead. There is no benefit to God when anyone dies, especially those who loved Him. Premature death is a real killer: it kills dreams, destroys families, and steals potential sons and daughters from God. Personally, I derive a great degree of peacefulness from knowing that when I die, I am going to sleep the soundest sleep I have ever slept. And when I wake up, totally refreshed, I will meet the Lord Jesus in the air, along with every other born-again believer who has lived or died since the day of Pentecost. That time could be days, months, or years away; no one knows. But, the next thing that any believer will be aware of after they die, is that moment when they are united with their Savior, the Lord Jesus Christ.

The Lake of Fire

When one dies, their body will corrupt, decay, or rot. Their soul or breath-life will have terminated. When one breathes their last breath, "that's all she wrote" for the soul of that person. It evaporates. A believer's spirit will return to God, who gave it. In terms of time, when a believers dies it will seem to them like they died and went immediately to the Lord, because they will be in the soundest sleep they have ever been in and they

---

[5] This account can be found in Heb 11:5. Later, in verse 13, it says, "These all died."

will not know anything else before that moment. But, to those loved ones whom they leave behind, it will seem like an eternity passes; they are those whom "death stings." In reality, everyone who has ever lived and died, with the exception of Jesus Christ, is in hell; the grave. Now there is no place, anywhere, where anyone is being tormented, for any reason. The only ones for whom a place of eternal torment is reserved are the Devil, the Beast, and the False Prophet. This place is called the Lake of Fire and it is discussed in Rev 20:10–15. In verse 14, after these three were cast in, death and hell were cast in, as well. Hell and the Lake of Fire are not one and the same. Many unbelievers will be cast into the Lake of Fire, but the Bible never says that they will be tormented day and night, as most of the Church believes. This is not the will of a just God. It is not God's will that anyone, at all, should be there. Everyone besides the Devil, the Beast, and the False Prophet, who are cast in the Lake of Fire, will be burnt to ashes and experience the second death.

2 Peter 3:9 says, "The Lord is not slack concerning his promise, as some men count slackness; but is longsuffering to us-ward, not willing that any should perish, but that all should come to repentance." God does not want anyone to perish in the Lake of Fire.

Romans 14:11–12 says, "For it is written, 'As I live, saith the Lord (YHWH,) every knee shall bow to me, and every tongue shall confess to God.' So then every one of us shall give account of himself to God." Not all will believe, but all will be called to give an account of their lives to God.

Finally, Philippians 2:9–11 says,

> Wherefore God also hath highly exalted him, and given him a name which is above every name: That at the name of Jesus every knee *should* bow, of things in heaven, and things in earth, and things under the earth; And that every tongue *should* confess that Jesus Christ is Lord, to the glory of God the Father.

This verse does not mean that everyone will eventually believe, whether they want to or not. The keyword here is "should." Five out of six top versions of the Bible say that we "should" bow and confess. This conditional does not mean that everyone will; but they should.

> For as in Adam all die, even so in Christ shall all be made alive. But every man in his own order: Christ the firstfruits; afterward they that are Christ's at his coming. Then cometh the end, when he shall have delivered up the kingdom to God, even the Father; when he shall have put down all rule and all authority and power. For he must reign, till he hath put all enemies under his feet. The last enemy that shall be destroyed is death. (1 Co 15:22–26)

This may be a hard truth for many to believe. Many would prefer to believe—and do—that their dead loved ones are looking down from heaven and watching us or just frolicking in fields of flowers. As I have said before, it really does not matter what you or I believe. All that matters is what the Word of God says. We can choose to believe it or not.

CHAPTER IX

THE GATHERING TOGETHER OF THE SAINTS

The *Parousia* and the *Episunagoge*

Since the Gospels of Matthew, Mark, Luke, and John fulfill the Law Administration, there is nothing written in them that pertains to the Gathering Together of the saints. What is written there applies to the Second Coming of Christ. The Second Coming, like the first, is primarily for Israel and is not to be confused with the Gathering Together of the Church of the Body. The chronology of the Rapture of the Church begins in 2 Thessalonians 2:1: "Now we beseech you, brethren, regarding the coming of our Lord Jesus Christ, and our gathering together unto him." There are two actions taking place here: his coming (*parousia*, 3952, arrival, advent) and our being gathered together (*episunagoge*)[1] "unto the Lord Jesus." The *parousia* is a multifaceted event that includes the Gathering Together, the coming of the Wicked One, and the Second Coming of Christ for Israel. The latter occurs about 7 years after the first two. This chapter will concern the Gathering Together, which will occur first.

---

[1] NT:1997 *episunagoogee, episunagoogees, hee*; a. a gathering together in one place, 2Th 2:1; b. (the religious) assembly (of Christians): Heb 10:25. Thayer's

The *episunagoge* is one part of the *parousia*. It is only for those who are born again of the spirit of God: the saved. Only the Church of God, will be "Gathered Together." Israel and its people are not raptured to meet the Lord in the air. *Episunagoge* comes from *episunago* (1996), which is a compound of *epi* (1909) and *sunago* (4863, to lead together, specifically, to entertain; implies hospitality).[2] *Sunago*, in turn, is a compound of *sun* (close union with) and *ago* (to bring or lead away; to accompany). The preposition *epi* governs three cases: the genitive, dative, and accusative, and it denotes superposition or one thing superimposed over another in time or space.[3] In the case of *episunagoge*, the prefix should be understood in the dative case, because the word "except" implies a condition: that the *episunagoge*, our gathering together, is resting, superimposed upon the *apostasia*, our departure from earth to meet the Lord Jesus in the air.

After the Gathering Together, the False Prophet—one of the antichrists—will be revealed or unveiled. 2 Thessalonians 2:2 continues, "That ye be not soon shaken in mind, or be troubled, neither by spirit, nor by word, nor by letter as from us, as that the day of Christ (Lord) is at hand." Here Christ is not translated from *Christos* (5547), but *kurios* (2962), which means lord. Furthermore, *kurios* is preceded by "the," but the article is not translated at all in the KJV. The NASU translates this section as "the day of the LORD," which is used 17 times in the Old Testament to refer to Yahweh's day, another part of the *parousia*. The day of the Lord Jesus (1Co 5:5; 2Co 1:14), of our Lord Jesus Christ (1Co 1:8), of Jesus Christ (Php 1:6), and of Christ (Php 1:10, 2:16) is a day of *rejoicing* (*kauchema*, 2745), not a time to be frightened. The day of the Lord Jesus is the *episunagoge*. The day of the LORD, Yahweh, is a time to be trembling with fear.

Paul was assuring the Thessalonians that the day of the LORD was not "at hand." He went on to give them the order of events that would

---

[2]   NT:4863 *sunago* (soon-ag'-o); from NT:4862 and NT:71; to lead together, i.e. collect or convene; specifically, *to entertain* (hospitably). Strong's

[3]   Bullinger, *The Companion Bible*, appendix 104 ix, page 149.

occur before that day. In 2 Thessalonians 2:3, Paul said, "Let no man deceive you by any means: for *that day* shall not come, except there come (*erchomai*, 2064) a falling away (a departure) first, *then* that man of sin be revealed, the son of perdition." *Erchomai*[4] is also used in 1 Thessalonians 1:10, where it says that we will be "delivered from the wrath to come," namely the Tribulation or the day(s) of the LORD. In 1 Thessalonians 5:2, Paul further says, "the day of the LORD so *cometh* as a thief in the night;" and in 2 Thessalonians 1:10, "When he shall *come* to be glorified with all his saints."

Above, the "falling away (*apostasia*, 646, the feminine of *apostasion*, a derivative of *aphistemi*, 868)," means to remove, to make stand off, or cause to withdraw. Acts 5:37 uses the word to describe the cause for Judas of Galilee's departure. In Acts 5, it is translated as "drew away." It is usually (10 out of 15 times) translated as "depart" or "departed." When used after verbs of motion, like *erchomai*, *apo* denotes separation: coming or going from one place to another.[5] "The preposition *apo* governs only one case (the Genitive), and denotes motion from the surface of an object, as a line drawn from the circumference; it stands in contrast with *ek*, which denotes a line drawn from the centre."[6]

> Now we request you, brethren, with regard to *the coming* of our Lord Jesus Christ, and our gathering together to Him, that you may not be quickly shaken from your composure

---

[4] NT:2064 *erchomai*; to come; 1. properly, a. of persons; universally, to come from one place into another, and used both of persons arriving, as in Mt 8:9; to come, i.e. to appear, make one's appearance, come before the public: Lk 3:16; 2. metaphorically, of *Christ's invisible return from heaven*. Thayer's

[5] NT:575 *apo*; *of, off from*, signifying separation, liberation, cessation, *departure*; used of separation; and 1. used of local separation, after verbs of motion from a place (of departing, fleeing, removing, expelling, throwing, etc. Luke 22:41; 2. used of the separation of apart from the whole; where of a whole some part is taken Mt 9:16; 3. of any kind of separation of one thing from another by which the union or fellowship of the two is destroyed; 4. of a state of separation. Thayer's

[6] Bullinger, *The Companion Bible*, appendix 104, page 148.

or be disturbed either by a spirit or a message or a letter as if from us, to the effect that the day of the Lord has come. Let no one in any way deceive you, for [it will not come] unless the apostasy comes first, then, (as *and* should be translated) the man of lawlessness is revealed, the son of destruction. NAS (2 Th 2:1–3)

The *apostasia* must come first, before the day of the Lord, which it does. It is pertinent to be aware of how translators have negatively translated or, in the case of the above passage, transliterated *apostasia* into apostasy. It does not signify a mass defection from the truth, as the translators make it out to be. It is not a falling away from the truth and there is nothing in the scriptures that supports such an understanding. It is no more an apostasy than *musterion* is a mystery. What Paul is saying here, to comfort believers, is, "don't worry about the day of the Lord, because we're all going to be taken out of here before that." Then, after that, the wrath of the days of the Lord will begin with the unveiling or revealing of "the son of destruction."

The *Apostasia* and the *Apokalupto* of the False Prophet

This brings us to another part of the *parousia,* the *apokalupto* of the son of perdition (*apoleia*),

> who opposeth and exalteth himself above all that is called God, or that is worshipped; so that he [as God] sitteth in the temple of God, shewing himself that he is God [...] whose coming (*parousia*) is after the working of Satan with all power and signs and lying wonders. (2 Th 2:4, 2:9)

This will be examined in a later chapter in more detail.

As we continue to explore what the *episunagoge* will be like, we read,

> But I would not [have] you to be ignorant, brethren, concerning them which are *asleep* (the dead believers that are in their graves),

that ye sorrow not, even as others which have no hope. For if we believe that Jesus died and rose again, even so them also which *sleep* in Jesus will God bring with him. For this we say unto you by [the] word of the Lord, that we which are alive *and* remain unto the coming of the Lord shall not prevent (precede) them which are asleep. For the Lord himself shall descend from heaven (but not to earth) with a shout, with [the] voice of the archangel, and with [the] trump of God: and the dead in Christ shall rise first: Then, we which are alive [and] remain (alive) shall be caught up together with them in [the] clouds, to meet the Lord in [the] air: and so shall we ever be with [the] Lord.

We will all be "airheads" then!

Paradise and Heaven

Those of us who remain alive at this phase of Christ's coming and those Christians who are dead in the grave, will meet the Lord Jesus in the air. In Eastern culture, when someone is expecting a visit, they do not wait for a knock on the door, they go out to meet their guest and then take them back to their home. Jesus does the same thing: he, and only he, meets us in the air and we go back with him from whence he came. From then on, wherever he goes, we go with him. Jesus will not come to the earth; no one else will see him and no one else will know it has occurred, except those who go to meet him in the sky.

There is yet another record of these events:

Behold, I shew you a secret; we shall not all sleep (die), but we shall all be changed, In a moment, in *the* twinkling of an eye, at the last trump: for *the* trumpet shall sound, and the dead shall be raised incorruptible, and we (who are alive and remain) shall be changed. For this corruptible (*phthartos,* the decayed dead) must put on incorruption (*apthartos*), and this mortal (*thnetos*), put on immortality (*athanasia*). So *when* this corruptible shall have put on incorruption, and this mortal shall have put on immortality, *then* shall be brought to pass (and not until then) the saying that is written, Death is swallowed up in victory. (1Co 15:51–54)

Please take a moment and look back at these three accounts in Paul's gospel. They make it abundantly clear that the dead believers are just that: dead and in the grave. If they were already in Heaven, as most of Christendom believes, how would they get back in the grave to be raised from the dead at the Rapture? And why would they? And why is there no account of such an action? I cannot, for the life of me, understand why pastors and teachers continue to speak of believers who die and go immediately to Heaven.

Oh, yes I can! Remember Luke 23:43: "And [Jesus] said unto him, Verily I say unto thee, To day shalt thou be with me in paradise?" It is amazing how much stock people put in a "comma." One of the reasons that the Bible is called the Word of God is because there were no chapters, verses, or punctuation. Scriptures were divided into chapters and verses where the translators felt it was appropriate. Punctuation was done the same way. Changing them in no way alters or adulterates the Word. If the above verse is translated completely and properly, Jesus would have been a "no show," since he was in the grave for the next 72 hours! "To day" he certainly was not in paradise. Was Jesus mistaken in thinking he was going to Paradise immediately after he died? I do not think so.

On the other hand, look at the difference it makes when the comma is placed after today: "Verily I say unto thee To day, shalt thou be with me in paradise." Or, as it is written, "Verily I say unto thee To day, with me shalt thou be in paradise." "With me" when? Whenever I am there! It was not that day or the day after, or the day after that. It still has not occurred! But, when it does, he will be there!

What did Jesus not say? Jesus did not say, "Today, thou shalt be with me in Heaven!" Well, are not Heaven and Paradise the same? Of course they are not! Yet, today Christians do not think they are any different. Heaven, or in the heavenlies, is always *above* the earth, while Paradise has been and always will be *on* the earth. Their logic (if you want to call it that) is, "What difference does it make?" I will tell you what difference it makes: the difference between us getting a lot of rewards at the Judgement Seat of Christ and getting *nada*! It is also a difference of 2000 years, plus or minus a hundred, but who is counting!

In biblical understanding, the minority of unclear or ambiguous verses on a subject must fit with the abundance of clear verses; not the other way around. The ambiguous verses are generally the result of how they have been translated or our lack of understanding of the culture.

One of the reasons that the Gathering Together is not considered a resurrection is because everyone involved is not dead. In the Resurrections of the Just and Unjust, everyone in that group which will be raised to life will have been dead, whereas, in the Rapture, some of those who are raised will still be alive.

When we meet the Lord in the air at the Rapture, it says that we will be ever with him. We will be with him and his messengers of power when he comes "taking vengeance in flaming fire" at the Second Coming for Israel.

Here are some other passages that mention the coming of Christ:

> So that ye become deficient in no gift (*charismata*), waiting for the coming (*apokalupsis*) of our Lord Jesus Christ: who shall also confirm you unto the end, that ye may be blameless in the day of our Lord Jesus Christ. God is faithful, by whom ye were called unto the fellowship of his Son Jesus Christ our Lord. (1Co 1:7–9)

> For, what is our hope, or joy, or crown of rejoicing? Are not even ye in the presence of our Lord Jesus Christ at his coming (*parousia*)? For, ye are our glory and joy. (1Th 2:19–20)

In the passage above, "ye" refers to those who have reconciled with God. I hope that by now it is clear how this day contrasts with the day of the LORD?

> And the very God of peace sanctify you wholly; and I pray God your whole spirit and soul and body be preserved blameless unto the coming (*parousia*) of our Lord Jesus Christ. (1Th 5:23)

Some peculiar words, which are not used in Paul's Epistles, show up in the next reference. This is a personal epistle, not a general epistle to the Church of God, which is evident in the first few verses of chapter one. James 5:7–8 says,

> Be patient therefore, brethren (those of the 12 Tribes of Israel, who were now born again) unto the coming (*parousia*) of the Lord. Behold, the husbandman waiteth for the precious fruit of the earth, and hath long patience for it, until he receive the early and latter rain. Be ye also patient; stablish your hearts: for the coming (*parousia*) of the Lord draweth nigh.

One can hardly imagine the patience that they must have had. How easy it would have been to give up hope. Yet, here we are, almost 2000 years later, still hoping for the same thing! The coming of Christ at the Gathering Together was their one, true hope and it remains ours.

> For, *the hope* which is laid up for you in heaven, whereof ye heard before in the word of the truth of the gospel. (Col 1:5)

> Looking for *that blessed hope*, and the glorious appearing (*epiphaneia,* manifestation) of the great God and our Saviour Jesus Christ. (Tit 2:13)

> Which *hope* we have as an *anchor* of the soul, both sure and stedfast. (Heb 6:19a)

The hope that one day we shall meet Christ in the air is the anchor of our lives, which keeps us from being "tossed to and fro and blown about with every wind of doctrine."

CHAPTER X

THE RESURRECTIONS

The Word "Resurrection" is not an Original Biblical Word

According to John 5:29, there will be two Resurrections. The difficulty in studying this subject is that the word "resurrection" is not derived from any original biblical language. Most of the words in the New Testament have a parallel word in the Old and vice-a-versa. "Resurrection" has no equivalent in the Old Testament. The word comes through Middle English (*resurreccion*) from Old French (*resurrection*), which, in turn, is derived from the Late Latin word *resurrectio*. The Latin word *resurgere* (past participle *resurrectus*) means to resurge.[1] Surge, which comes from the Latin verb *surgere*, means "to lead straight up, rise." It is significant to note that the origin of "resurrection" is in neither the Hebrew nor Greek from which most of the Bible is translated. In reality, "resurrection" is not a biblical word at all. The Greek word that is translated as "resurrection" is *anastasis,* which means "a raising up, standing up again, especially after death." *Anastasis* is a compound of the prefix *ana* (up) and *histemi* (to stand). It is highly doubtful that the "resurrection" of Jesus Christ will ever be replaced by the "standing up again" of Jesus Christ, but that is what it really was.

---

[1] *The American Heritage Dictionary of the English Language* (New York: American Heritage and Houghton Mifflin, 1970).

In order for a true resurrection to occur, there are mitigating circumstances. Ezekiel 37:12–14 says,

> Therefore prophesy and say unto them, Thus saith the Lord GOD; Behold, O *my* people, I will open your graves, and cause you to come up (ascend) out of your graves, and *bring you* into the land of Israel. And ye shall know that I am the LORD, when I have opened your graves, O my people, and brought you up out of your graves, And shall put my spirit in you, and ye shall live, and *I shall place you* in your own land: then shall ye know that I the LORD have spoken it, and performed it, saith the LORD.

This passage speaks of the Resurrection of the Just. This is going to be extremely difficult for God to do if there is no one in the graves, as common belief has it. God is not going to open their graves so that they can ascend into heaven. Rather, He is going to place them in their own land! This will begin the fulfillment of the covenant God made with Abram in Genesis 15:18: "In the same day the LORD made a covenant with Abram, saying, Unto thy seed have I given this land, from the river of Egypt unto the great river, the river Euphrates."

In Daniel 12:1–2, we read,

> And at that time shall Michael stand up, the great prince which standeth for the children of thy people (Israel): and there shall be a time of trouble (the Great Tribulation) such as never was since there was a nation [even] to that same time: and at that time (the end of the Great Tribulation) thy people (Israel) shall be delivered, every one that shall be found written in the book and many of them that *sleep* in the dust of the earth shall *awake,* some to everlasting life, and some to shame *and* everlasting contempt.

Here, there are clearly two totally different *Awakenings*. The dead are called asleep and the opposite of being asleep is being awake! John 5:29 confirms the two true Awakenings:

> Marvel not at this: for the hour is coming, in the which all *that are in the graves* shall hear his voice, and shall come forth; they that have done good, unto resurrection (*anastasis*) of life; and they that have done evil, unto resurrection (*anastasis*) of damnation (a thousand years transpires between these two events). (28–29)

> But when thou makest a feast, call the poor, the maimed, the lame, the blind: and thou shalt be blessed; for they cannot recompense thee: for thou shalt be recompensed at the resurrection (*anastasis*) of the just. (Lk 14:13–14)

> Have hope toward God, which they themselves also allow; there shall be a resurrection [of the dead], both of the just and unjust. (Ac 24:15)

Notice that, in the passage above, the words "of the dead" were added by the translators. There is no need to supply this information, because there can only be one "of the dead." This is why the Gathering Together of the Church cannot be considered a resurrection, because some believers will still be living.

In John 11:23–24, "Jesus saith unto her, Thy brother shall rise again (*anistemi*). Martha saith unto him, I know that he shall rise again (*anistemi*), in the resurrection (*anastasis*) at the last day." *Anistemi* is also used in Luke 24:46 and John 20:9 to describe the future rising of Jesus from the dead. *Egeiro* is used in Matthew 28:7, Luke 24:6, and John 21:14, after he had risen. Jesus represented the *anastasis/quwts*, the future Awakenings of the Just and Unjust, to Israel, not to us. We will not all be asleep at the Rapture of the Church. Just as the *anastasis/quwts* is Israel's hope, the *episunagoge* is our *hope*.

Quwts, the Corresponding Hebrew Word to *Anastasis*

In both the Old and the New Testament the "resurrection" is described as waking up from being asleep. "Awake (*quwts*),"[2] means exactly that, along "with the idea of abruptness in starting up from sleep." Jesus could have just as easily said, "I am the Awakening and the life." He certainly would not have said, "I am the resurrection," as Martha would have had no idea what he was talking about (and I do not think Jesus spoke Latin).[3]

More Scriptures relating to the *Anastasis*

> Paul, a servant of Jesus Christ, called an apostle, separated unto [the] gospel of God (which he had promised afore by his prophets in [the] Holy Scriptures), concerning his Son, who was made (*ginomai*, came into being) of [the] seed of David according to flesh (*sarx*, bodily, as opposed to of the soul or spirit), declared Son of God with power, according to [the] spirit of holiness, by *standing up* (*anastasis*) from the dead. (Ro 1:1–4)

> Now if Christ be preached that he rose from [the] dead, how say some among you that there is no *standing up* (*anastasis*) of the dead? But if there be no standing up (*anastasis*) of the dead, then is Christ not risen: and if Christ be not raised (*egeiro*, awakened), your faith [is] vain; ye are yet in your sins; then they also which are *fallen asleep* (*koimao*, deceased) in Christ are perished. If in this life only we have *hope* in Christ, we are of all men most miserable. AT (1Co 15:12–13, 15:17–19)

> But, now is Christ *awakened* (*egeiro*) from dead; [the] firstfruit of them that *slept* (*koimao*), for, since by man came death, by man came also *standing up* (*anastasis*) from the dead. For, as

---

[2] OT:6974, Strong's

[3] For more passages containing the word *quwts*, see Job 14:12, Ps(s) 7:6, 35:23, 57:8, and Isa 26:19.

in Adam all die, even so in Christ shall all be made alive. But every man in his own *order:* Christ the firstfruit; afterward they that *are* Christ's at his coming (*parousia*). AT (1Co 15:20–23)

Here, what is pertinent is that not all will be made alive at the same time. Order (*tagma*) is in succession: Christ first; then us at the Rapture; then those in the first Resurrection; and lastly, those in the second Resurrection. So far, these *anastasis(es)* will take place over 2987 years!

Then Cometh the End

> Then, [cometh] *the end* (*telos*),[4] when he, Jesus, shall have delivered up the kingdom to God, and Father; when he, Jesus, shall have put down all rule and all authority and power. For he, Jesus, must reign (for 1000 years) till he, God, hath put all enemies under his, Jesus', feet; last (*eschatos*, final) enemy that shall be destroyed is death. For he hath put all things under his feet. *But* when he saith, all things are put under, [him it is] manifest that he, God, is excepted, whom did put all things under him. And when all things shall be subdued unto him (the Father), then shall the Son also himself be subject unto him who put all things under him, that God may be all in all. AT (1Co 15:24–28)

Death is the final enemy to be destroyed. It is not destroyed at the Rapture. It does receive a sort of slap in the face then, nor at the first Resurrection, but dying continues, for some, through the Millennial Kingdom, when Jesus will reign as King for 1000 years, according to Revelation 20:6. However, in the passage above it says that he must reign

---

4   NT:5056 *telos* (tel'-os); from a primary tello (to set out for a definite point or goal); properly, the point aimed at as a limit, i.e. (by implication) the conclusion of an act or state (termination [literally, figuratively or indefinitely], result [immediate, ultimate or prophetic], purpose); specifically, an impost or levy (as paid). Strong's

until the last enemy is destroyed. Death is not destroyed until Revelation 20:14–15: "And death and hell were cast into the lake of fire (this is the second death). And whosoever was not found written in the book of life was cast into the lake of fire." From this we know that some were still dying during Jesus' reign, because death was not destroyed until the end of his reign. We will see more on this subject later.

CHAPTER XI

EVIL ENTITIES OF THE GREAT TRIBULATION

Characteristics of that Person of Wickedness

The administration (*oikonomia*) of the Great Tribulation will begin immediately after the Gathering Together of the Church of God, which is the last event of the *Oikonomia* of Grace, the Secret Administration. The first event of the new administration is the unveiling of "that person of wickedness," as recorded in 2 Thessalonians 2:3b, where it says, "that man of sin (*anomia*) be revealed, the son of perdition." Perdition (*apoleia*) means utter destruction or ruin. The phrase "son of perdition" serves to adjectivally describe this individual's destructive nature. He or she is "that person (*anthropos*), human being of wickedness, lawlessness" (2 Th 2:3). Here are some of their characteristics:

1. Opposes and goes against God and all He represents.
2. Raises oneself over and above God.
3. Sits in the temple of God.
4. Demonstrates or exhibits him/herself as God.
5. Operates the working energy of Satan (2 Th 2:9).
6. Demonstrates all power (*dunamis*).

7. Demonstrates supernatural signs.

8. Performs lying (*pseudos*, to deceive by falsehood), wonders, miracles.

9. Manifests delusions of injustice; destroying fully, because they failed to receive (*dechomai*) the love (*agape*) of the truth.

Many believe that this individual is *the* Antichrist. They certainly are an antichrist. Before we jump to any conclusions, let us look at what the Bible says on the subject.

The spirit of Antichrist

What follows is everything the Bible has to say about antichrists. To be an antichrist, one must deny or reject that Jesus is the Christ (*Christos*), the anointed one, the Messiah, the saviour of mankind.

> Little children, it is [the] last time: and as ye have heard that antichrist shall come, even now are there *many* antichrists; whereby we know that it is [the] last time. They went out from us, but they were not of us; for if they had been of us, they would have continued with us: but, that they might be made manifest that they were not all of us. (1Jn 2:18–19)

> Who is a liar but he that denieth that Jesus is the Christ? He (she or it) is antichrist, that denieth the Father and the Son. (1Jn 2:22)

> And every spirit that confesses not Jesus, is not of God and this is that of antichrist, whereof ye have heard that *it* should come; and even now already is *it* in the world. (1Jn 4:3)

> For *many* deceivers (impostors or misleaders, i.e. antichrists) are entered into the world, who confess not [that] Jesus Christ is come in [the] flesh.[1] (2Jn 7)

---

[1] Here, the words "Christ is come in the flesh" were added by the translators.

The article "the" is very important. It is a definite article.[2] It does not appear in any of the verses that apply to the word "antichrist." Even though many people say that the "man of sin" is *the* antichrist, the Bible does not support the theory of a single Antichrist. There is not just one antichrist, but *many*. The plural pronouns in the preceding verses are proof of that. Most telling are the multiple uses of "it" in 1 John 4:3. There are ten words in the passages above, which imply plurality. 1 John 4:3 concerns the "spirit" of antichrist and refers to it as "it (*esti,* 2076)." The man of sin is definitely *an* antichrist.

The book of Revelation sheds some light on who this person may be. In order to understand who the antichrists are, it is important to know who they are not. Thus, we will look at the characteristics or attributes of each. Basically, there are three evil entities in the book of Revelation: the Dragon, the Beast, and the False Prophet (Rev 16:13). In Revelation 19:20 and 20:10, these three are cast into the Lake of Fire, where they are to be eternally tormented. As previously discussed, the Dragon is that Old Serpent, the Devil, or Satan: "And the great dragon was cast out, that Old Serpent, called the Devil, and Satan, which deceiveth the whole world: he was cast out into the earth, and his angels were cast out with him (Rev 12:9)."

The Beast (*therion,* 2342) is a dangerous animal. *Therion* comes from the word *thera,* which denotes a wild animal, as in game; hunting, i.e. (figuratively) destruction. *Thera* is used in Romans 11:9 to describe a trap set for men, in conjunction with the words "snare" and "stumblingblock." Many mistakes are made in interpreting literal things in the Bible as figurative and figurative things as literal. The beasts mentioned in Revelation 4 and 6 are a different: *zoon* (2226) is a living thing or being; an animal. The word is a derivative of *zao* (2198), to live or to have life. However, these references do not concern us here.

The first *therion* beast is associated with "the bottomless pit," as demonstrated in Revelation 11:7. Here, the Beast ascends out of the bottomless

---

[2] NT:3588 *ho* (ho); including the feminine *he* (hay); and the neuter *to* (to); in all their inflections; the def. article; the (sometimes to be supplied, at others omitted, in English idiom): KJV - the, this, that, one, he, she, it, etc. Strong's

pit, makes war on two witnesses, and kills them. In Revelation 13:1–4, it rises up out of the sea with the name of blasphemy upon its head. Its power and authority derive from the Dragon, Satan. This beast had ten horns and seven heads. On each of its horns was a diadem, a kingly ornament. Each of its seven heads had a blasphemous name. One of the heads was wounded to death, but was healed. "All the world wondered (admired), after him" (Rev 13:3). What complicates the understanding of who these beasts are, is that the first one mentioned does not appear on the scene until the second half of the Tribulation. This can be seen in Rev. 11:7, when this beast kills the two witnesses, who had been prophesying for the previous 42 months, according to 11:2.

Characteristics of the First Beast: the Political Antichrist

Therion is used six times in Revelation 13:1–4.

1. It arose from the sea and had ten horns and seven heads. (13:1)
2. A kingly crown was upon each horn and blasphemous names were upon its seven heads.[3] (13:1)
3. The dragon gave it its power (*dunamis*), throne, and great (*megas*) authority. (13:2)
4. The whole earth followed after the beast, because it was healed of a deadly wound. (13:3)
5. They, all the world, worshipped the dragon and the beast, prostrated themselves before them. (13:4, 13:8)
6. It was given a mouth speaking haughty and blasphemous things. (13:5)
7. It was allowed to exercise its authority (*exousia*) for 42 months. (13:5)
8. It spoke blasphemous things against God, his name, his habitation: those who resided in heaven. (13:6)

---

[3] One may only blasphemy God, the Spirit (Mt 12:31).

9. It was allowed to make war on the saints and subdue them. (13:7)

10. It was given authority over every tribe, people, language, and nation. (13:7)

11. All the inhabitants will worship it: everyone whose name has not been written in the book of life of the Lamb. (13:8)

12. Its calculated number (*arithmos*), as reckoned up, is number of a person, six hundred threescore six. (13:18)

The Beast's throne is described in Revelation 17:

1. It was and is not and is about to ascend out of the bottomless pit and go to destruction (*apolei*). (17:8a, 17:11)

2. All that dwell on the earth, whose names were not written in the book of life, from the conception of the world, will be amazed when they see the beast, because it was and is not and is to come. (17:8b)

3. It is an eight king which belongs to the seven. (17:11)

Characteristics of the Second Beast, the False Prophet, the Spiritual Antichrist

In Revelation 13:11, another (*allos*) different beast rose out of the earth and spoke as a dragon:

1. It had two horns like a lamb and spoke as with fascination.

2. It exercises all the authority (*exousia*) of the first beast, on its behalf and compels all the inhabitants of the earth to worship the first beast. (13:12)

3. It performs great wonders (*semeion*), remarkable signs. (13:13).

4. It makes fire come down from heaven, for all to see. (13:13)

5. It deceives everyone by means of its miracles (the same word, *semeion*). (13:14)

6. It told the inhabitants that they should make an image (*eikon*, likeness, statue, profile, representation, icon) to the first beast.

7. It had the power to give spirit (*pneuma*) to the image. (13:15)

8. That the image could both speak and cause to be killed (*apokteino*), slay those who refused to worship the likeness of the first beast.

9. And it makes all to receive a mark (*charagma*, a scratch or etching, like a stamp, worn as a badge) upon their right hand or foreheads. (13:16)

10. So that no person would be able to buy or sell anything. (13:17)

11. Without the mark, the stamp, etching, or engraven, that is, name of the beast or the number (*arithmos*, 706, as reckoned up) of its name (*onoma*, 3686,[4] from a presumed derivative of the base of 1097[5])

It is easy to see that these are two different entities, simply because one has ten horns, while the other has only two. I believe that this is all the descriptive information we have about these two *theiron* beasts. The reason I am spending so much time on this is because of what it says in Revelation 19 and 20:

> And the beast was taken, and with him the false prophet that
> wrought miracles before him, with which he deceived them that
> had received the mark of the beast, and them that worshipped

---

[4] NT:3686 *onoma, onomatos, to*; name by which a person or a thing is called, and distinguished from others; 1. universally: used of proper names, Mk 3:16; 2. used for everything which the name covers, everything the thought or feeling of which is roused in the mind by mentioning, hearing, remembering, the name. Thayer's

[5] NT:1097 *ginooskoo*; universally: 1. to learn to know, come to know, get a knowledge of; 2. to know, understand, perceive, have knowledge of; a. to understand: with the accusative, Lk 18:34; b. to know: Lk 12:47; 3. by a Hebraistic euphemism. In particular: to become acquainted with, to know, a. the one, true God, in contrast with the polytheism of the Gentiles: Ro 1:21; b. his blessings, Php 3:10; c. *gnoonai . . . ta tou pneumatos*; the things which proceed from the Spirit, 1 Co 2:14. Thayer's

his image. These *both* were cast alive into a lake of fire burning with brimstone. (19:20)

And (1000 years later) the devil that deceived them was cast into the lake of fire and brimstone, where the beast and the false prophet are, and shall be tormented day and night for ever and ever. (20:10)

From the scriptures relating to the beasts, it is clear that one is political in nature, while the other is more along the lines of spiritual. What the False Prophet of Revelation 19:20, the second beast of Revelation 13:13, and the man of sin of 2 Thessalonians 2:9 all have in common is that they are all attributed with the ability to perform lying signs—miracles and wonders—while the first beast is not. Thus, they are all spiritual in nature. It is my conclusion that these three are actually one: by name, the False Prophet, the Spiritual Antichrist.

The Beast, its Image, and the Number of its Name

What else does the Word say about the first beast, the one who is political in nature? Just as the Devil and the False Prophet have several descriptive names or aspects, so does the 666 beast.

And the third angel followed them, saying with a loud voice, If any man worship 1) the beast and 2) his image, and receive 3) mark in his forehead, or in his hand. (Rev 14:9)

And they have no rest day nor night, who worship the beast and his image, and whosoever receiveth the mark of his name. (Rev 14:11)

And I saw as it were a sea of glass mingled with fire: and them that had gotten the victory over the beast, and over its image, and over the number of its name, stand on the sea of glass, having harps of God in their hands.[6] (Rev 15:2)

Again, Revelation 19:20 mentions the Beast, the mark, and its image. Therefore, the first beast is constituted by:

1. the beast itself
2. the image of the beast, made by people
3. the mark of the beast, and
4. the number of its name

Something that has recently become very popular in business marketing, is the use of quick reading (QR) codes. These codes are currently two-dimensional, with two layers of information. They are designed to be read by an application that can be downloaded to smart phones. At some point into the Tribulation, no one will be able to sell or buy anything without the mark of the Beast. It is very interesting that QR codes were introduced to us on the sell side of the equation. I am not saying that this is the mark of the Beast, but I can see how it could be a predecessor to it. Here is some of what Wikipedia says about QR codes:

> In the USA, QR code usage is expanding. During the month of June 2011, according to one study, 14 million mobile users scanned a QR code or a barcode. Some 58% of those users scanned a QR or bar code from their home, while 39% scanned from retail stores; 53% of the 14 million users were men between the ages of 18 and 34. While the adoption of QR codes in some markets has been slow to begin (particularly in markets such as the United States, where competing standards such as Data Matrix exist), the technology is gaining some

---

[6] The phrase "and over his mark" was added by the translators. There are many verses of scripture like this, where pronouns do not refer to the previous noun, but refer to the subject. The previous nouns are the beast, etc. The beast, etc. were not holding the harps of God; those who had gotten the victory were. See also 1Jn 5:20.

traction in the smartphone market. Many Android, Nokia, Blackberry handsets, and the Nintendo 3DS, come with QR code readers installed. QR reader software is available for most mobile platforms. Moreover, there are a number of online QR code generators which enable users to create QR codes for their own needs.[7]

Risks: Malicious QR codes combined with a permissive reader can put a computer's contents and user's privacy at risk. QR codes intentionally obscure and compress their contents and intent to humans._They are easily created and may be affixed over legitimate QR codes. On a smartphone, the reader's many permissions may allow use of the camera, full internet access, read/write contact data, GPS, read browser history, read/write local storage, and global system changes.

Risks include linking to dangerous websites with browser exploits, enabling the microphone/camera/GPS and then streaming those feeds to a remote server, exfiltrating sensitive data (passwords, files, contacts, transactions), and sending email/SMS/IM messages or DDOS packets as part of a botnet, corrupting privacy settings, stealing identity, and even containing malicious logic themselves such as JavaScript or a virus. These actions may occur in the background while the user only sees the reader opening a harmless webpage.[8]

More Scriptures on the Political Antichrist

The following passages will lend a little more understanding and insight into this beast. Remember, the Beast had ten horns:

---

[7] I just got an invoice from my insurance company and the QR code on it is 1/4 inch square.

[8] "QR code," Wikipedia, http://en.wikipedia.org/wiki/QR_code.

And the ten horns which thou sawest are ten kings, which have received no kingdom as yet; but receive power as kings one hour with the beast. These have one mind, and shall give their power and strength unto the beast. These shall make war with the Lamb, and the Lamb shall overcome them: for he is Lord of lords, and King of kings: and they that are with him are called, and chosen, and faithful. (Rev 17:12–14)[9]

And the fifth [angel] poured out his bowl upon the throne of the beast; and its kingdom was plunged into darkness (blindness); people gnawed their tongues in agony, and blasphemed the God of heaven because of their pains and their sores, and repented not of their deeds. And the sixth [angel] poured out his bowl upon the great river Euphrates; and its water was dried up, in order to prepare the way for the kings from [the] east. And I saw three devil spirits like frogs [come] out of the mouth of the dragon, and out of the mouth of the beast, and out of the mouth of the false prophet. For they are the spirits of devils, working miracles, which go forth unto the kings of [the earth and] the whole world, to gather them to the battle [of that] great day of God the Almighty. And they assembled them together into a place called in the Hebrew tongue Armageddon. (Rev 16:10–14)

Then I saw the beast and the kings of the earth with their armies, gathered to make war against the rider on the horse and his army. And *the beast* was seized and with it the *false prophet* who had performed in its presence the signs by which he deceived those who had received the mark of the beast, and those who worshipped its image. These two were thrown alive into the lake of fire that burns with sulfur. And the rest were killed by the sword of the rider on the horse, the sword proceeded out of his mouth: and all the birds were gorged with their flesh. (Rev 19:19–21)

---

[9]   Remember 1 Thessalonians 4:17: "so shall we ever be with the Lord."

The Final Battle with the Devil
Thrown into the Lake of Fire

> Then, I saw an angel coming down from heaven, holding in his hand the key of the bottomless pit and a great chain. He seized the dragon, that ancient serpent, who is the Devil and Satan, and bound *him* (singular) a thousand years, And threw him into the bottomless pit, and locked and sealed it over him, so that he should deceive the nations no more, until the thousand years were ended. After that he must be let out for a little while. (Rev 20:1–3)

> (1000 years later:) And the devil who had deceived them was thrown into the lake of fire and sulfur, where the beast and the false prophet *were*, and they will be tormented day and night for ever and ever. (And only they!) (Rev 20:10)

We know that the two *theiron* beasts of Revelation are entirely different. The first rose up from the sea and, the second, the earth. And, as far as I can tell, the second beast preceded the first, since it was the False Prophet who was revealed (*apokalupto*)[10] at, or soon after, the Rapture in 2 Thessalonians 2:3. You can see from the definition of *apokalupto*, that this individual was already here, but that their true identity was unknown or "covered up." The False Prophet paved the way for the Beast, like John the Baptist did for our Lord Jesus. The False Prophet, the spiritual Antichrist, did not seek to be worshipped, but compelled all the people to worship the other beast, the political Antichrist. The False Prophet performed great *semeion* (wonders) and even had the power to give spirit (*pneuma*, life). The first beast is not afforded either of these abilities.

---

[10] NT:601 *apokaluptoo*; 1. properly, to uncover, lay open what has been veiled or covered up; to disclose, make bare: Ex 20:26; 2. metaphorically, to make known, make manifest, disclose, what before was unknown. Thayer's

Chapter XII

THE COLD, HARSH REALITY OF THE GREAT TRIBULATION

The Survivors

Once the Grace Administration has terminated with the Gathering Together, the Tribulation Administration will begin. The hard, cold reality of this age is that in order to be allowed into the Millennial Kingdom of Christ, one will need to stay faithful unto the end: the end of your life or the end of this 7-year period. There is no more being born again of incorruptible seed; no more salvation by grace; no more holy spirit created within. As the spirit was available to the Old Testament believers, so will it be to those of this age and time, conditionally, by measure, and depending upon on one's faithfulness; not sealed in.

Those who make it through the Tribulation alive and are admitted into the Millennial Kingdom will continue the current life cycle. They will not have eternal or everlasting life, as the born-again will have. They will continue to live as they always have, with the exception of Jesus Christ being their King. They will marry, have children, die, and so on and so forth. To clarify, I am not talking about those who are a part of the Resurrection of the Just, but those who believe during, and survive the Great Tribulation, for one. They will have 1000 years to populate the Kingdom and they must do a pretty good job, or else Satan, when loosed after that 1000 years, would not have anyone to deceive one last time, according to Revelation 20:8: "Gog and Magog."

The Gospels, and especially the book of John and the book of Revelation, flow together, since the apostles thought that Christ was going to come back and set up his Kingdom relatively soon after his Ascension. They had no idea that Jesus himself was going to pick Judas' replacement and that the Secret Administration was going to be revealed to Paul. Those who choose not to believe during the Grace Administration, will soon understand what an incredible opportunity they passed up. Matthew 24 describes what those left behind after the Rapture of the Church have to look forward to: verses 5–7 describe "the beginning of sorrows." Here, the word "sorrows" is the same word that means childbirth and the travail associated with it: panging to be delivered.

> Then (after the beginning of sorrows) shall they deliver you up to be afflicted (pressured to recant your faith) and shall kill you: and ye shall be hated of all nations for my name's sake. And then shall many be offended (*skandalizoo*, entrapped to sin) and shall betray one another, and shall hate one another. And many false prophets shall rise, and shall deceive many. And because wickedness shall abound (it abounds because all of us in whom the spirit of God lived are gone; we were the light of the world and darkness is once again upon the earth), the love (*agape*) of many shall wax cold. But he that shall endure unto [the] *end*, the same shall be saved, (delivered). (Mt 24:9–13)

Today, believers do not have to persevere to the end in order to be saved. You can have the Promise of Salvation right now by making Jesus your Lord and believing that God raised him from the dead. You do not even have to stay committed to him through the end of your life in order to be saved, but it would behoove you not to. This is another reason why Matthew, Mark, Luke, and John cannot be talking to us, the saints.

When ye therefore shall see the abomination of desolation, spoken of by Daniel the prophet (11:31; 12:11), stand in [the] holy place, (whoso readeth, let him understand:) then let them which [be] in Judaea flee into the mountains: let him which [is] on the housetop not come down to take [any thing] out of his house: neither let him which [is] in the field return back to take his clothes. And woe unto them that are with child, and to them that give suck in those days! But pray ye that your flight be not in the rainy season, neither [on the] sabbath: for then shall be *great tribulation*, such as was not since [the] beginning of the world, no, nor ever shall be. And except those days should be shortened, there should no flesh be saved: but for the elect's sake (faithful of the Israelites) those days shall be shortened. Then if any man shall say unto you, Lo, here [is] Christ, or there; believe [it] not. For there shall arise *false* Christ's, and *false* prophets, and shall shew *great signs and wonders*; insomuch that, if [it were] possible, they shall deceive the very elect. (Mt 24:15–24)

This is not something I would like to look forward to, yet, believe it or not, many Christians do. Many think "grace" is too easy. But, there are also many who want to work for their salvation; many who want to pay the price Jesus paid to give it to us, freely. It does not matter, because if you are born again, you are not going through the Great Tribulation, even if you want to. This just goes to show how unsound Christians can be. It all comes about by failure to rightly divide scripture. Why would anyone have a "desire" to go through this if they did not have to?

Daniel's Prophesy

The abomination of desolation is also mentioned in Mark 13:14, but the words "spoken of by Daniel the prophet" were added by the translators. It is pretty much a given that this was also what Mark was talking about. But, what is this abomination of desolation anyway?

Daniel 11:31: "And arms shall stand on his part, and they shall pollute the sanctuary of strength, and shall take away the daily [sacrifice], and they shall place the abomination that maketh desolate." Here, the abomination is *shiqquwts* (OT:8251, disgusting, i.e. filthy, especially idolatrous). "Desolate" is *shamem* (OT:8074, to stun, i.e. devastate, or, figuratively, to stupefy, appall). In the Greek, abomination is *bdelugma* (946), a foul, detestable thing. "Desolation" is *eremosis* (2050, despoliation), which comes from *eremos* (2048, by implication, waste). Whatever this idol is, it is certainly sickening to YHWH.

Some of the "abominations" mentioned in the Old Testament are Ashtoreth, the principal female deity of the Phoenicians, who represented love and fertility; Milcom, the god of the Ammonites and Phoenicians, to whom some Israelites sacrificed their infants; Kemosh, also known as Molech, the god of the Moabites, subduer, also identified with Baalzebub, Mars, and Saturn (1Ki 11:5–8). These idols were erected by Solomon on the tops of the hills that surrounded Jerusalem. This should serve as a sober reminder to all of us that no one, no matter how wise he may be, is immune to serving other gods. I used to have a book in my library called *Babylon, Mystery Religion: Ancient and Modern*, by Ralph Woodrow. He explains a lot about "the groves and high places and abominations," of which Daniel speaks.

Daniel 12:11–13 goes on to say,

> And from the time [that] the daily [sacrifice] shall be taken away and the abomination that maketh desolate set up, [there shall be] a thousand two hundred and ninety days. Blessed is he that waiteth, and cometh to [the] thousand three hundred and five and thirty days. But go thou thy way till the end [be:] for thou shalt rest, and *stand* in thy lot at the end of the days (at the resurrection of the Just.)

Figuring out how long this is can be taxing, because there are not really 365 days in a year; there are actually only 364, based on 7 days in a week and 52 weeks in a year. However you want to look at it, the first 1290 days are approximately 3.54 years. The second 1335 days are approximately 3.67 years, totaling 7.21 years. These two time periods relate, relatively, to the first and second halves of the Great Tribulation. During the first half, possibly 30 days after the False Prophet is revealed or unveiled, Revelation 11:3 says, "And I will give [power] unto my two witnesses, and they shall prophesy a thousand two hundred [and] threescore days, clothed [in] sackcloth." Using the same method of calculation as above, 1260 days is approximately 3.46 years. Sackcloth generally represents mourning and grief. At the same time, what we read about in Daniel has taken place and the False Prophet has been performing their lying signs and wonders and preparing the people to worship the coming Beast and its image, which the people would eventually make, in addition to receiving the mark of the Beast and the number if its name. There is little doubt about what the two witnesses were prophesying.

Revelation 11:7 says, "And when they [shall] have finished their testimony, the beast that ascendeth out of the bottomless pit shall make war against them, and shall overcome them, and kill them." After the Beast kills them, they lay dead in the street for 3.5 days, while the people rejoice over them. Revelation 11:10 says, "And they that dwell upon the earth shall rejoice over them, and make merry, and shall send gifts one to another; because these two prophets tormented them that dwelt on the earth." The people considered the prophesying of these two to be torment. People generally receive prophets like this; it is nothing new.

> And after three days and an half [the] spirit of life from God entered into them, and they stood upon their feet; and great fear fell upon them which saw them. And they heard a great voice from heaven saying unto them, Come up hither. And they ascended up to heaven in a cloud; and their enemies beheld them. And the same hour was [there] a great earthquake, and the tenth part of the city fell, and in the earthquake were slain of men seven thousand: and the remnant were affrighted, and gave glory to the God of heaven.

This is an obvious end of the first half, approximately 3.5 years of the Great Tribulation.

The Beast that killed the two witnesses is not mentioned again until Revelation 13. As previously mentioned, many of the things that are recorded in the book of Revelation are not chronological. Try to imagine all the things that were revealed to John. In Revelation 13:5, it says, "And there was given unto him a mouth speaking great things and blasphemies; and power was given unto him to continue forty and two months." It is remarkable that God had John write 42 months! That is 3.5 years, marking the beginning of the second half of the Great Tribulation!

The Day(s) of the LORD (YHWH)

This study begins with the first usage of these words, in Isaiah. But, before getting to that, I want to point out that 1 day is not just a 24-hour period. Unlike the Rapture, which occurs "in a moment, in the twinkling of an eye," the "day (*yowm*, OT:3117)" figuratively means a space of time, according to Strong's. Matthew 24 describes those days of the Lord, known as the Great Tribulation, and says this about them:

> For then shall be great tribulation, such as was not since the beginning of the world to this time, no, nor ever shall be. And except those *days* should be shortened, there should no flesh be saved: but for the elect's sake those *days* shall be shortened. (Mt 24:21–22)

For the elect's sake, not for ours; thank God we will not be there. We cannot be "the elect" about whom Matthew speaks, because we will not be on the earth at this time.

> For the day of the LORD, (YHWH,) of hosts [shall be] upon every one [that is] proud and lofty, and upon every one [that is] lifted up; and he shall be brought low: [...] and the loftiness of man shall be bowed down, and the haughtiness of men shall be made low: and the LORD alone shall be exalted in that *day*. And the idols he shall utterly abolish. And they shall go into the holes of the rocks, and into the caves of the earth,

for fear of the LORD, and for the glory of his majesty, when he ariseth to shake terribly the earth. In that day a man shall cast his idols of silver, and his idols of gold, which they made [each one] for himself to worship, to the moles and to the bats. (Isa 2:12, 2:17–20)

Behold, the day of the LORD (YHWH) cometh, cruel both with *wrath* and fierce anger, to lay the land desolate: and he shall destroy the sinners thereof out of it. For the stars of heaven and the constellations thereof shall not give their light: the sun shall be darkened in his going forth, and the moon shall not cause her light to shine. And I will punish the world for [their] evil, and the wicked for their iniquity; and I will cause the arrogancy of the proud to cease, and will lay low the haughtiness of the terrible. I will make a man more precious than fine gold; even a man than the golden wedge of Ophir. Therefore I will shake the heavens, and the earth shall remove out of her place, in the *wrath* of the LORD of hosts (the one from which we are saved in 1Th 5:9), and in *the day* of his fierce anger. (Isa 13:9–13)

The earth shall quake before them; the heavens shall tremble: the sun and the moon shall be dark, and the stars shall withdraw their shining: And the LORD shall utter his voice before his army: for his camp [is] very great: for [he is] strong that executeth his word: for the day of the LORD [is] great and very terrible; and who can abide it? (Joel 2:10–11)

The great day of the LORD [is] near, [it is] near, and hasteth greatly, [even] the voice of *the day* of the LORD: the mighty man shall cry there bitterly. That day [is] a day of *wrath* (overflowing rage), a day of trouble and distress, a day of wasteness and desolation, a day of darkness, misery and gloominess, wickedness, a day of clouds and thick darkness, as of a lowering sky, a day of the trumpet (*shophar*), and alarm, battle-cry, against the fenced cities, and against the high towers (figuratively, rulers). And I will bring distress upon men, that they shall walk like blind men, because they have sinned against the LORD: and their blood shall be poured out as dust, and their flesh as the dung. Neither their silver nor their gold shall be able to deliver them in the day of the LORD's *wrath*; but the whole land shall be devoured by the fire of his jealousy: for he shall make even a speedy riddance of all them that dwell [in] the land. (Zep 1:14–18)

It should be crystal clear from these passages that this is YHWH's time, the time of the One True God, who passes judgment on the earth and its inhabitants. No one who has previously believed in the name of His Son will be on the earth during this time. Only those who have rejected Jesus Christ will be there. Remember these words of John: "Whosoever denieth the Son, the same hath not the Father: (but) he that acknowledgeth the Son hath the Father also" (1Jn 2:23). To reject the Son is to reject the Father, as well.

Looking at usages of "the day of the Lord" in the New Testament, we see that in 1 Corinthians 5:5, the word "Jesus" at the end of the verse was erroneously added by the translators: "To deliver such an one unto Satan for the destruction of the flesh, that the spirit may be saved in the day of the Lord [Jesus]." In 2 Corinthians 1:14, "the day of the Lord Jesus" is a day of rejoicing: "As also ye have acknowledged us in part, that we are your *rejoicing*, even as ye also are ours in the day of the Lord Jesus." No one is rejoicing in the day of YHWH. 1 Thessalonians 5:2 properly associates the day of YHWH with destruction:

> For yourselves know perfectly that [the] *day of the Lord* so cometh as a thief in [the] night. [For] when they shall say, Peace and safety; then *sudden destruction cometh* upon them, as travail [upon] a woman with child; and they shall not escape. (1 Th 5:2–3)

2 Peter 3:10 also refers to the day of YHWH and relates it to destruction:

But [the] day of the Lord will come as a thief [in the night;] in [the] which the heavens shall pass away [with] a great noise, and [the] elements shall melt with fervent heat, [the] earth also and the works [that are] therein shall be burned up.

Nothing like this takes place on the day of the Lord Jesus.

There is only one uncorrupted reference to the day of the Lord Jesus, which is a day of rejoicing. The day of YHWH is in no way the same or in any way similar to it. Jesus does have a part in the day of the LORD: it is the fulfillment of the prophesying that was received from Yahweh and reported by the prophets. He is the one opening the seven seals of the book he took out of YHWH's hand (Rev 5:7).

Revelation 6:1–8:1 describes the contents behind each of the seven seals. In verse 6:15, we read what Isaiah prophesied in Isaiah 2:19:

And the kings of the earth, and the great men, and the rich men, and the chief captains, and the mighty men, and every bondman, and [every] free man, hid themselves in the dens and in the rocks of the mountains; and said to the mountains and rocks, Fall on us, and hide us from [the] face of him that sitteth on the throne and from the wrath of the Lamb (as the one who executed it, see Joel 2:11) For the great day of his wrath is come; and who shall be able to stand? (Rev 6:15–17)

This is what they said. The Lamb executed or carried out the wrath of the Father, YHWH. Jesus Christ always represented God; he always did the Father's will. They related the wrath of he that sitteth on the throne to the Lamb, since he was the one carrying it out.

The Sealing of the 144,000

Before the seventh seal is unsealed and before any damage to the earth or sea (Rev 7:3) could take place, something of particular importance needed to take place: the "sealing" or marking of the 144,000 people of the 12 Tribes of Israel. They were to be marked with the seal of the living God

(Rev 7:2) on their foreheads. Once this was accomplished, the seventh seal was opened and John saw seven angels with seven trumpets standing before God (Rev 8:1). Then, another angel, besides these seven, threw fire on the earth (Rev 8:5), commencing the actual events of the wrath of God. When these events began, we do not know. But, I believe that they began after the two witnesses were slain and raised from the dead. The prophesying of these two prophets was the last best chance for the inhabitants of the earth to believe, before the actual wrath of God began. Revelation 9:4 speaks of the significance of the marking of the 144,000 and it also demonstrates that the day of the LORD is not one 24-hour period:

> And it was commanded them that they should not hurt the grass of the earth, neither any green thing, neither any tree; but only those men which have not the seal of God in their foreheads. And to them it was given that they should not kill them, but that they should be tormented five months: and their torment was as the torment of a scorpion, when he striketh a man. (Rev 9:4–5)

The first of these seven angels sounded his trumpet in Revelation 8:7 and the last in verse 11:15:

> And the seventh angel sounded; and there were great voices in heaven, saying, The kingdoms of this world are to become (*ginomai,* 1096) [the kingdoms] of our LORD, and of his Christ (Messiah); and shall reign for ever [and] ever. And the four and twenty elders, which sat before God on their seats, fell upon their faces, and worshipped God, saying, We give thee thanks, [O] Lord God Almighty, which art,[1] and wast,[2] [and

---

[1]   NT:1510 *eimi* (i-mee'); the first person singular present indicative; a prolonged form of a primary and defective verb; I exist (used only when emphatic): KJV - am, have been, it is I, was. Strong's

[2]   NT:2258 *en* (ane); imperfect of NT:1510; I (thou, etc.) was (wast or were): KJV - agree, be, have (+charge of), hold, use, was (-t), were. Strong's

art to come], because thou hast taken [to thee] thy great power
and hast reigned. (Rev 11:15–17)

Again, this takes place in the future, not now. The Messiah is not yet
ruling in his kingdom; his Second Coming has not yet even occurred. It
is unclear who the 24 elders are, but the only ones in heaven at this time,
besides God, Jesus Christ, and the heavenly host of angels, are us, the
raptured believers.

> And I saw another sign in heaven, great and marvelous, seven
> angels who had seven plagues, which are the last, because in
> them the wrath of God is finished. NAS (Rev 15:1)

> And I heard a loud voice from the temple, saying to the seven
> angels, Go and pour out the seven bowls of the wrath of God
> into the earth. NAS (Rev 16:1)

This continues through verse 17, when the last, or seventh, vial or
bowel is poured out, signifying the end of the wrath of God and the "day"
of the LORD.

God has blessed those who choose to believe, during this day and time,
with so much grace. Just consider all we escape! At the culmination of the
"day of the LORD," we will make our appearance with the Lord Jesus coming
in the clouds.

The Second Coming of Christ

As I have previously demonstrated, Jesus did not know about "the days
and times" in which you and I now live. God kept the Grace Administration
a secret from everyone. Much like the scripture passage that many have been
quoting lately, "only the Father knows" or knew (Mk 13:32). When Jesus
prophesied of his return to earth, it was for Israel's sake; they are the ones to
whom he was sent.

The Second Coming of Christ is foremostly described in the Gospels and
is specifically addressed to Israel. The reason it is addressed to Israel is as stated

above: no one knew about the Grace Administration; it was a secret that only the Father knew (see Ro 16:25; Eph 3:3–5, 3:9; Col 1:26). As such, that which is written in the Gospels cannot be referring to the Rapture of the Church of the Body of Christ, which is part of the secret about which none of the original 12 Apostles knew anything prior to the revelation given to Paul.

1 Thessalonians 3:13 says, "To the end he may stablish your hearts unblameable in holiness before God, even our Father, at the coming of our Lord Jesus [Christ] *with* all his saints." It will be awfully difficult to come with him, if we are not already there! I think this little four-letter word, "with," is one of the biggest in the Epistles of Paul. We come with him!

> When the Lord Jesus shall be revealed from heaven *with* his mighty angels (messengers, envoy) in flaming fire taking vengeance on them that know not God, and that obey not the gospel of our Lord Jesus [Christ:] who shall be punished [with] everlasting destruction from [the] presence of the Lord and from the glory of his power; when he shall come to be glorified in (*en,* with) his saints, and to be admired with (*en)* all them that believe (because our testimony among you was believed) in that (*ekeinos*) day. (2Th 1:7b–10)

"That day," when we return *with* our Lord Jesus, will be the last event that culminates in the Great Tribulation. Jesus spoke of it in Mark 13:32: "But of *that (ekeinos) day* and that hour knoweth no man, no, not the angels which are in heaven, neither the Son, but the Father."

In approaching the subject of the Second Coming, we should be sure to keep in mind all the dissimilarities of the Rapture.

> Immediately *after* the tribulation of *those (ekeinos) days* shall the sun be darkened, and the moon shall not give her light, and the stars shall fall from heaven, and the powers of the heavens shall be shaken (like Isaiah and Joel said): And *then* shall appear the sign of the Son of man in heaven: and *then* shall all the tribes of the earth mourn (*kopto*), and they shall see (*optanomai,* with eyes wide open), the Son of man coming (*erchomai*) in

141

the clouds of heaven with power and great glory. And he shall send his angels with great reverberation (*salpigx*) and they shall gather together his elect from the four winds, from one end of heaven to the other. AT (Mt 24:29–31)

For these be days of vengeance, [that] all things which are written may be fulfilled. Woe unto them with child, and to them that give suck, in those (*ekeinos*) days! for there shall be great distress in the land, and *wrath* upon this people (like Zephaniah said). And they shall fall by the edge of the sword, and made captive among all nations: and Jerusalem shall be trodden down of Gentiles (*ethnos*), until times of the Gentiles be fulfilled. And there shall be signs in sun, and in the moon, and in the stars; and upon the earth distress of nations, with perplexity: sea and loud vibration (*salos echos*); Men's hearts failing them for fear, and anticipation of those things which are coming on the earth: for the powers of heaven shall be shaken (*saleuo*, from *salos*, above). And then shall they see (*optanomai*) the Son of man coming in a cloud with power and great glory. And when these things begin to come to pass, get up, and lift up your heads; for your, Israel's, redemption draweth nigh. AT (Luke 21:22–28)

This is altogether quite a different scene than that of the Rapture.

But as the days of Noe, so shall the coming of the Son of man be. For as in the days that before the flood they (everyone except Noe and his family) were eating and drinking, marrying and having children (*gaster*), until [the] day that Noe entered into the ark, And knew not until the flood came, and *took* all away; so shall also the coming of the Son of man be. Then shall two be in the field; one shall be *taken*, and other left; Two grinding at the mill; one shall be *taken*, and other left. AT (Mt 24:37–41)

What is commonly missed here is that when the flood came, those who were still eating, drinking, and marrying, died. Verse 39 above says that the flood "*took* (them) all away."

> Likewise it was in the days of Lot; they did eat, they drank, they bought, they sold, they planted, they builded; but the same day Lot went out of Sodom it rained fire and brimstone from heaven, and destroyed all. Thus shall it be in the day when the Son of man is revealed. In that (*ekeinos*) day, he which shall be upon the housetop, and his stuff in the house, let him not come down to take it away: and he in the field, let him likewise not return back. Remember Lot's wife. Whosoever shall seek his life shall lose it; and whosoever shall lose shall preserve it. I tell you, in that night there shall be two in one bed; the one shall be *taken*, and the other shall be left. Two shall be grinding together; the one shall be taken, and the other left. Two men shall be in the field; the one shall be *taken*, and the other left.[3] AT (Lk 17:28–36)

> But in those days, *after* that tribulation, the sun shall be darkened, and the moon shall not give her light, And the stars of heaven shall fall, and the powers that *are* in heaven shall be shaken (*saleuo*.) And then shall they see the Son of man coming in the clouds with great power and glory. And then shall he send his angels, and shall gather together his elect from the four winds, from the uttermost part of the *earth* to the uttermost part of heaven. Verily I say unto you, that this generation shall not pass, till all these things be done. Heaven and earth shall pass away: but my words shall not pass away. *But* of that day and that hour knoweth no man, no, not the angels which are in heaven, neither the Son, but the Father. (Mk 13:24–27, 13:30–32)

---

[3] Verse 36 does not appear at all in the oldest MSS, like Nestle, but does appear in the Textus Receptus.

This is further proof that God the Father did not tell Jesus the secret He kept, otherwise Jesus would not have made the statements he did in verses 30–31 above. Possibly realizing this, he covered himself in verse 32 by saying that there were some things that only the Father knew. I think that Jesus truly believed that he would be returning soon after his Ascension into heaven. None of the four previous Gospel passages mentions anything about "the *episunagoge* or the *apostasia*," as mentioned in Thessalonians.

The Battle of Armageddon

This last account of Jesus' Second Coming culminates with the Battle of Armageddon:

> And I saw heaven opened, and behold a white horse; and he that sat upon him was called Faithful and True, and in righteousness he doth judge and make war. His eyes were as a flame of fire, and on his head were many crowns; and he had a name written, that no man knew, but he himself. And he was clothed with a vesture dipped in blood: and his name is called The Word of God. And the armies which were in heaven followed him upon white horses, clothed in fine linen, white and clean (we are with him). And out of his mouth goeth a sharp sword, that with it he should smite the nations: and he shall, in the future, rule them with a rod of iron: and he treadeth the winepress of the passionate wrath of Almighty God. And he hath on [his] vesture and on his thigh a name written, KING OF KINGS, AND LORD OF LORDS. And I saw an angel standing in the sun; and he cried with a loud voice, saying to all the fowls that fly in [the] midst of heaven, Come [and] gather yourselves together unto the supper of the great God; that ye may eat [the] flesh of kings, and [the] flesh of captains, and [the] flesh of mighty men, and [the] flesh of horses, and of them that sit on them, and [the] flesh of all, both free and bond, both small and great. And I saw the beast

(the political Antichrist), and the kings of the earth, and their armies, gathered together to make war against him that sat on the horse, and against his army. And the beast was taken, and with him the false prophet that wrought miracles before him, with which he deceived them that had received the mark of the beast, and them that worshipped his image. These both were cast alive into a lake of fire burning with brimstone. And the remnant were slain with the sword of him that sat upon the horse, which proceeded out of his mouth: and all the fowls were filled with their flesh. (Rev 19:11–21)

In Luke 4:18–19, it says that our Lord, Jesus Christ, stood up in the synagogue and read Isaiah 61:1–2a. He closed the book and sat down after reading just the first half of the second verse. The second half of that verse says, "and the day of vengeance of our God; to comfort all that mourn." During his first coming, Jesus did not come to proclaim this; but, at his Second Coming, he definitely will. Take this as a word to the wise: "For we know Him who said, Vengeance is Mine, I will repay. And again, *the* LORD will judge His people. *It is* a terrifying thing to fall into *the* hands of the living God" NAS (Heb 10:30–31).

Everyone has a choice. Some will fear their parents, their religious leaders, or their ancestry more than they will fear God and His written Word. If I were not already saved, nothing would stop me from doing so. We have now seen the alternative of making Jesus your Lord. It is a simple choice between eternal life and the second death; "I call heaven and earth to record this day against you, that I have set before you life and death, blessing and cursing: therefore choose life, that both thou and thy seed may live" (Dt 30:19).

CHAPTER XIII

OTHER ASPECTS OF
THE BOOK OF REVELATION

Written to Israel's Bond-Servants

> [The] Revelation of Jesus Christ, which God gave Him to show
> to His bond-servants, the things which must soon take place;
> and He sent [and] communicated [it] by His angel to His bond-
> servant John, who testified the word of God even the testimony
> of Jesus Christ, to all that he saw. NASU (Rev 1:1–2)

In the passage above, from the beginning of the book of Revelation, God
gives this revelation to Jesus Christ. God then sent an angel (probably
Gabriel; see Lk 1:19; Da 8:16 and 9:21) to reveal this revelation to His
bond-servant, John, who then testified to the Word of God and even the
testimony of Jesus Christ, as he saw them. It is difficult to distinguish
what the angel is doing, what Jesus is doing, and what God is doing.
This is why it is so important to understand the first few verses of every
book in the Bible. As I have mentioned before, the Apostles expected this
revelation to come to pass in their lifetime, because they were unaware
of the Administration of the Sacred Secret; they did not know about the
Rapture of the Church before the Great Tribulation.

The 12 Apostles were a very special group, because they were the first to believe and follow the Lord Jesus. They were the leaders of the first generation of believers, who lived during the two administrations of the Law and of the Secret. As such, they will have a special place in Christ's Kingdom when it is set up, after the Great Tribulation:

> Ye are they which have continued with me in my temptations. And I appoint unto you a kingdom, as my Father hath appointed unto me; that ye may eat and drink at my table in my kingdom, and sit on thrones judging the twelve tribes of Israel. (Lk 22:28–30)

Primarily Addresses the Great Tribulation

Before continuing on to Revelation 1:4, it is pertinent to emphasize what a church is and is not. In the Bible, a church is not a building with a cross on the top of it; it is not any physical building. The word "church" is *ekklesia*, which means a gathering of *people*, called out for some specific purpose or reason; an assembly. In Acts 19:32, the *ekklesia* was a mob that set out to kill Paul and his companions. In short, an *ekklesia* is a gathering of *people* that come together for any number of reasons. The 99 percenters could accurately be called an *ekklesia*.

Revelation 1:4 says that God's revelation is addressed to the seven *ekklesias* in Asia and that the revelation John received was about the LORD, YHWH's, day, which, as we already know, is the time period nearing the end of the Great Tribulation.[1]

> John to the seven churches which [are] in Asia: Grace [be] unto you, and peace, from Him which is, and which was, and which is to come; and from the seven spirits which [are] before his throne; *and from* Jesus Christ, [who is] the faithful witness, [and] the first begotten of the dead, and the prince of the kings

---

[1] Revelation 8 sets the beginning of these days.

of the earth. Unto him that loved us, and washed us from our sins in his own blood. (Rev 1:4)

YHWH is the "Him which is, and which was and which is to come" in this passage. This is more clearly laid out in Revelation 1:8. What follows are lists of all the words used in this study, as they relate to YHWH and to Jesus Christ, as well as other important subjects:

Attributes of *YHWH*

1. Him which is, and which was and which is to come. (Rev 1:4, 1:8, 4:8)
2. The Alpha and the Omega (i.e. the beginning and the ending—not in texts). (Rev 1:8, 21:6, 22:13)
3. God and Father of Jesus Christ. (Rev 1:6)
4. Glory and dominion forever and ever. (Rev 1:6)
5. The Lord, YHWH, the Almighty. (Rev 1:8, 4:8)
6. Holy, Holy, Holy is the Lord God. (Rev 4:8)
7. He alone is Holy. (Rev 15:4)
8. He sits on the throne. (Rev 4:9–10, 5:1, 5:13, 19:4)
9. Lives in perpetuity, forever [and] ever. (Rev 4:9–10)
10. Only one to be Worshipped. (Rev 4:10, 7:11, 11:16, 14:7, 15:4, 19:4, 19:10, 22:9)
11. Our Lord and our God. NASU, NRSV (Rev 4:11)
12. Worthy to receive glory, honor and power. (Rev 4:11)
13. For He created all things and because of His will they existed and were created. (Rev 4:11)
14. Had a book with seven seals in his right hand. (Rev 5:1)
15. To him who sits on the throne be blessing, honor, glory, and power. (Rev 5:13)
16. Will wipe away tears in the Everlasting Kingdom. (Rev 21:4)
17. Salvation and glory and power belong to Him. (Rev 19:1)
18. His judgments are true and righteous. (Rev 19:2)

19. Whoever overcomes during the great Tribulation, He will be their God and they will be His sons. (Rev 21:7)

Attributes of Jesus Christ

1. The Faithful Witness. (Rev 1:4)
2. The firstborn of the dead. (Rev 1:4)
3. The *future* ruler of the kings of the earth. (Rev 1:4)
4. Him who loved and released us from our sins by his blood. (Rev 1:4)
5. Made unto us, Israel, royal priests. (Rev 1:6, 5:10)
6. He cometh amidst the clouds. (Rev 1:7)
7. Every eye will see him (Rev 1:7). But, no one sees him at the Rapture.
8. All the tribes of the earth will mourn (*kopto*), beat their breast in grief. (Mt 24:30) This does not happen at the Rapture.
9. Out of his mouth came a sharp two-edged sword. (Rev 1:16, 2:12, 2:16, 19:15, 19:21)
10. His countenance shined like the strength of the sun. (Rev 1:16)
11. The first (*protos*) and the last (*eschatos*) and the living one. NASU, NRSV (Rev 1:17)
12. Was dead and now alive forevermore. (Rev 1:18)
13. Has the keys of death and Hades, the grave. (Rev 1:18)
14. Usually standing, never sits on a throne until after the Battle of Har-magedon. NASU (Rev 3:20, 5:6, 14:1)
15. The Lion of the tribe of Judah, the root of David. (Rev 5:5)
16. Called the Lamb. (Rev 5:6, 5:8, 5:12–13, 6:1, 6:16, 7:9–10, 7:14, 7:17, 21:14, 21:22–23, 22:1, and 12 other places)
17. Took the book with seven seals out of the right hand of him who sat on the throne. (Rev 5:7)
18. Worthy to take the book, because he was slaughtered and by his blood he ransomed for God every tribe and tongue and people and nation. (Rev 5:9)

19. And to the Lamb be blessing, honor, glory and power. (Rev 5:13)
20. On his Robe and thigh he has a name written, KING OF KINGS AND LORD OF LORDS! (Rev 17:4, 19:16)
21. Rode a White horse. (Rev 19:11)
22. Called Faithful and True. (Rev 19:11)
23. In righteousness he judges and wages war. (Rev 19:11)
24. His name is called the Word (*logos*) of God. (Rev 19:13)
25. He tramples the winepress of the passionate wrath of Almighty God. (Rev 19:15)

The Raptured Believers

After the Rapture, we will ever be with our Lord Jesus; wherever he is, we will also be. A few of the places where this is mentioned specifically:

> These shall make war with the Lamb, and the Lamb shall overcome them: for he is Lord of lords, and King of kings: and they that [are] with him [are] *called, and chosen, and faithful.* (Rev 17:14)

> And I saw the beast, and the kings of the earth, and their armies, gathered together to make war against him that sat on the horse, and against *his army.* (Rev 19:19)

> And I beheld, and I heard [the] voice of many angels round about the throne and the beasts (*zoon*) and the elders: and the number of them was myriads of myriads, and thousands of thousands. NASU (Rev 5:11)

The Bond-Servants of God

> Revelation of Jesus Christ, which God gave Him to show to His *bond-servants,* the things which must soon take place; and He sent and communicated it by His angel to His *bond-servant* John. NASU (Rev 1:1)

And I saw another angel ascending from the rising of the sun, having the seal of the living God; and he cried out with a loud voice to the four angels to whom it was granted to harm the earth and the sea, saying, Do not harm the earth or the sea or the trees until we have sealed the *bond-servants* of our God on their foreheads. And I heard the number of those who were sealed, one hundred and forty-four thousand sealed from every tribe of the sons of Israel (12,000 from each tribe). NASU (Rev 7:2–4)

Then I looked, and behold, the Lamb was standing on Mount Zion, and with Him one hundred and forty-four thousand, having His name and the name of His Father written on their foreheads. And I heard a voice from heaven, like the sound of many waters and like the sound of loud thunder, and the voice which I heard was like the sound of harpists playing on their harps. And they sang a new song before the throne and before the four living creatures and the elders; and no one could learn the song except the one hundred and forty-four thousand who had been purchased from the earth. These are the ones who have not been defiled with women, for they have kept themselves chaste. These are the ones who follow the Lamb wherever He goes. These have been purchased from among men as first fruits to God and to the Lamb. And no lie was found in their mouth; they are blameless. NASU (Rev 14:1–5)

And they sang the song of Moses, the bond-servant of God, and the song of the Lamb. NASU (Rev 15:3)

There will no longer be any curse; and the throne of God and of the Lamb will be in it, and His bond-servants will serve Him; they will see His face, and His name will be on their foreheads. NASU (Rev 22:3–4)

The First Awakening with the Sheep and Goat Judgment

Everything previously covered from the book of Revelation occurs before the "then" in the following verse:

> When the Son of man shall come in his glory, and all the [holy] angels (*aggelos*, messengers) with him, *then* shall he sit upon [the] throne of his glory. And before him shall be gathered all nations: and he shall separate them one from another, as a shepherd divideth his sheep from the goats: and he shall set the sheep on his right hand, but the goats on the left. Then shall the King say unto them on his right hand, Come, ye blessed of my Father, inherit the kingdom prepared for you from the foundation of the world. (Mt 25:31–34)

So, who are the sheep and the goats? The Rapture took place 7 years prior to this, so born-again Christians cannot be a part of either of these two groups. The *anastasis* of the Just will take place in and around this time, so the just likewise cannot be a part of either of these two groups. The Unjust cannot be a part, because their *anastasis* will not come for another 1000 years, or so. The White Throne Judgment is also after the Millennial Kingdom. Matthew 25:32 provides some clue: it says that they are from all nations (*ethnos*) or foreign races.

The key to the identity of the sheep and the goats is in understanding the "then" of verse 31. A lot can take place before a "then." "Then" is an adverb that modifies a verb, which in this case is "sitting down." Often times it is the little overlooked words in the Bible that make the difference between truth and error. It is also noteworthy that, when a king "sits down," it is a sign of completeness; he is not going to sit down if there is any unfinished business for which he must remain upright.

In 2 Thessalonians 1:7–10 there is another record of the Son of man coming *with* someone:

> And to you who are troubled rest with us, when the Lord Jesus shall be revealed from heaven with his mighty angels (*aggelos*).

CHAPTER XIV

CHRONOLOGY
THE CHRONOLOGY OF MAJOR EVENTS NEAR THE END OF THE *OIKONOMIA* OF GRACE, THROUGH THE TRIBULATION *OIKONOMIA*, THROUGH THE MILLENNIAL KINGDOM *OIKONOMIA*, TO THE EVERLASTING KINGDOM OF THE NEW HEAVEN, NEW EARTH, AND NEW JERUSALEM

1. Our Gathering Together unto the Lord Jesus Christ (2Th 2:1, 2:3). The Church of God's appearance before the Judgment Seat (*bema*) of Christ to be rewarded or suffer loss (1Co 3:13–15; 2Co 5:10).
2. The revealing, unveiling of the person of wickedness (2Th 2:3).
3. The Spiritual Antichrist, who is called the False Prophet, sets out to deceive with *pseudos* signs (2Th 2:4–12).
4. The 144,000 Bond-servants of the 12 Tribes of Israel are sealed (Rev 7:4).
5. The two witnesses (*martus*), who prophesy 1260 days (3.5 years), standing before the Lord of the earth (Rev 11:3–4).
6. The Political Antichrist, the Beast, kills the two witnesses; power was given to him to continue 42 months (3.5 years), the last half of the Great Tribulation (Rev 13:1–10).

7. It was given unto the Beast, by the Old Serpent, to make war with the *hagios* and overcome them (Rev 13:7).

8. The Dragon, the Beast, and the False Prophet gather together the kings of the whole world for the battle at Har-Magedon (Rev 16:14, 16:16; see also 17:14 and 19:17–21).

9. The raptured believers accompany the Lord Jesus to the battle of Armageddon: the Second Coming (Mt 25:31a; 2Th 1:7–10).

10. The Beast and the False Prophet are taken and cast into the Lake of Fire; the rest are slain; fowls gorge themselves with the flesh of the slain (Rev 19:20–21).

11. The Dragon, that Old Serpent, who is the Devil and Satan, is bound a thousand years (Rev 20:2).

12. *Then*, the Son of man will sit down on his glorious throne (Mt 25:31b).

13. The Sheep and Goat Judgment for those who were sealed, those who believed, and those who did not, during the Great Tribulation (Rev 20:4–6; see also Rev 7:14–15: the sheep will minister day and night in the temple for 1000 years).

14. The first Resurrection, that of the Just: they shall be priests of God and of Christ and shall reign with Christ for 1000 years (Rev 20:6).

15. The fulfillment of YHWH's promise to Abram of inheriting the land (Eze 37:12–14; Da 12:1–2a).

16. Satan is loosed to deceive the nations once again; final battle with Gog and Magog (Rev 20:7–9).

17. Satan and his counterparts are cast into the Lake of Fire, where the Beast and the False Prophet have been for the past 1000 years; they, and only they, will be tormented day and night, forever and ever. All others will be incinerated, immediately (Rev 20:10).

18. The White Throne Judgment and the second *anastasis* (Rev 20:11–13).

19. The second death: death, the grave, and those not found written in the book of life are cast into the Lake of Fire and are burnt up (Rev 20:14–15).

20. The New Heaven, the New Earth, and a New Jerusalem; the Everlasting Kingdom, where all the saints shall live together, eternally. The full promise of salvation is complete to all who qualify (Rev 21–22).

21. The marriage supper of the Lamb and the bride, the Lamb's wife (Rev 19:9, 21:9).

CHAPTER XV

FOR MY MUSLIM AND JEWISH FRIENDS

The One True God

Prior to the birth of the Messiah, Jesus of Nazareth, all there was, was YHWH, the One True God and His heavenly host. There were many false god's, just as there are today, but only One True God. Muslims believe that everything that is addressed to Israel in the Bible, is addressed to them. They attribute most everything that is said about YHWH in the Bible, to Allah. They believe that the Comforter that Christ spoke of is actually Mohammed. They believe that Jesus was *a* son of God, as opposed to *the* Son of God. They view the Qur'an as more sacred than the Bible. These are sincere, but counterfeit beliefs. As I have said throughout this book, it does not matter what anyone believes if what you believe does not align itself with the Gospel of God in Christ Jesus, as revealed to the Apostle Paul.

From what I have ascertained, the two biggest problems Muslims have with Christianity are the worship of Jesus and Jesus' birth as the *only begotten* of the Father. I could not agree more with the former. Only YHWH is to be worshipped. The true worshippers are supposed to worship in *spirit*. When we worship "in spirit," our understanding is unfruitful., The Bible teaches us that speaking in tongues is *unto* God (1Co 14:2). John once attempted to physically worship the Messenger (Rev 19:10, 22:9), but the Messenger prevented him from doing so and told him to "worship God." On occasion, other men, in their desire to show respect, fell down at the feet of others and physically worshipped them. But true worship is "in spirit," not in body, nor, for that matter, in mind either. Philippians 3:3 says that those of us who have been *spiritually* circumcised, "worship God in the spirit and rejoice in Christ Jesus." Nowhere in the Bible are any believers told to worship anyone but YHWH.

The *monogenetic* Son of God

On the second point—that of Jesus being God's only begotten (*monogenes*, 3439) Son—the word *monogenes* means one of a kind, only born, or sole.[1] Jesus is one-of-a-kind; there is no other like him. *Monogenes* is not only translated as "only begotten," it is also translated as "only son" (Lk 7:12). "only *daughter*" (Lk 8:42), and "only *child*" (Lk 9:38). *Monogenes* comes from the words *monos* (3441), meaning sole or single, and *ginomai* (1096), which means to cause to be, become, or come into being (existence).[2] *Monos* is used 48 times and *ginomai* is used 673 times in the New Testament. At that point in time, Jesus was the *monogenes* Son of God. I don't know any Muslims who would not agree with this. They love Jesus and probably appreciate him more than most Christians do, for who he truly was, what he did, and what he continues to do, today. Translators have mis-translated many words in the Bible.

The *genesis* of Jesus Christ

When one makes Jesus their Lord, God creates His seed in that individual. As was discussed in Chapter III, we become born again of

---

[1]   NT:3439 *monogenees, monogenes; single of its kind, only* (Thayer's); from NT:3441 and NT:1096; *only-born, i.e. sole.* Strong's

[2]   NT:1096 *ginomai*; to become, i.e. *to come into existence*, begin to be, receive being: absolutely. Thayer's

incorruptible "seed" (1 Peter). The word "seed (*spora*)" implies parentage.[3] *Spora* and *sperma*[4] both come from *speiro* (4687) and *spao* (4685). It is easy to see that these words are the roots of the English words spore and sperm, which are both used to describe reproduction; the sowing of seed. To gain a better understanding of the birth of Christ, consider the usage of words in following passage: "An account of the *genesis* (1078)[5] of Jesus the Messiah, son of David, son of Abraham" (Mt 1:1). Here, *genesis* is a noun that means origin, source, or beginning; it comes from the word *ginomai* (1096): to come into being. Similarly, "And Jacob begat (*gennao*, 1080) Joseph the husband of Mary, of whom was born (*gennao*) Jesus, who is called Christ or Messiah" (Mt 1:16).

Matthew 1:18 should read, "The beginning, *genesis* (with one "n"), or origin of Jesus Christ happened this way," not, "Now the birth (*gennesis*, with a double "n") of Jesus Christ happened in this way."[6] The earliest and best manuscripts agree in introducing the passage with the words "The beginning." Some manuscripts have "<1078>" accompanying the word *genesis*. The reason for this is that other manuscripts use the word *gennesis* (1083). One thing that further sets these two words apart is that *genesis* can also mean creation. *Genesis* and "now" also flow with the context of Matthew 1:1.

> Now the beginning (*genesis*, 1078) of Jesus Christ was on this wise: his mother Mary was espoused to Joseph, before they came together, she was found with child of holy spirit (no article *the*). But [while] he thought on these things, behold,

---

3   NT:4701 *spora* (spor-ah'); from NT:4687 (speiro); a sowing, i.e. (by implication) parentage. Strong's

4   NT:4690 *sperma* (sper'-mah); from NT:4687; something sown, i.e. seed *(including the male "sperm")*; by implication, offspring; specifically, a remnant (figuratively, as if kept over for planting). Strong's

5   NT:1078 *genesis, geneseoos, hee*; 1. source, *origin*; 2. used of birth, nativity, in Mt 1:18; 3; of that which follows origin, viz. *existence*, life Jas 3:6. Thayer's

6   Bart D. Ehrman, *The Orthodox Corruption of Scripture: The Effect of Early Christological Controversies on the Text of the New Testament.* (Oxford: Oxford University Press, 1993).

[the] angel of the Lord appeared unto him in a dream, saying, Joseph, son of David, fear not to take Mary *thy wife*: for that which is *conceived* in her is of[7] holy spirit (no article *the*). (Mt 1:18, 1:20)

It says this is the beginning, the *genesis,* of Jesus Christ. You either believe it or you do not. If you do not, then there is no reason to believe anything else the Bible has to say.

"For that which is conceived (*gennao,* a verb, 1080) in her is of [the] holy ghost." First of all, there is no article "the" in these texts. When there is no article, there should be no capital letters either. It should read: "for that which is to be born in her is of holy spirit." "That which is conceived" is the single word *gennao* (1080, from *ginomai,* 1096), meaning to procreate, regenerate, or engender. In the Bible, it is variously translated as "begat," "should be born," "were born," "been born," "shall bear," "bear," "brought forth," "be born (again)," "was born (Moses)," "is delivered," "which gendereth," "is born (us who believe)," "free born (Paul)," "is begotten (us)," etc. In Matthew 1:20, it should have been translated as "that which is to be born," instead of "conceived." This distinction will become more succinct in the following verses.

And, behold, thou shalt conceive (*sullambano,* 4815)[8] in *thy* womb, and bring forth (*tikto*) a son, and shalt call his name JESUS. He shall be great, and shall be called [the] son of the Highest: and [the] Lord God shall give unto him the throne of his father David: And he shall reign over the house of Jacob for ever; and of his kingdom there shall be no end. Then said Mary unto the angel, How shall this be, seeing I know not (never had intercourse with) a man? And the angel answered, saying

---

7   NT:1537 *ek* (ek) or *ex* (ex); a primary preposition *denoting origin* (the point whence action or motion proceeds), *from, out of* (place, time, or cause; literal or figurative; direct or remote. Strong's

8   NT:4815 *sullambano* (sool-lam-ban'-o); from NT:4862 and NT:2983; to clasp, i.e. seize (arrest, capture); specifically, *to conceive* (literally or figuratively); by implication, to aid: KJV - catch, conceive, help, take. Strong's

unto her, holy spirit shall come upon thee, and power (*dunamis,*
1411) of the Highest shall overshadow thee: therefore also [that]
holy thing which shall be born [of thee] shall be called [the] son
of God. (Lk 1:31–35, AT)

First, notice that this passage is in the future tense, while the previous
one from Matthew was in the past tense. Second, notice that the word
translated as "conceive" is totally different than the word used in Matthew.
Sullambano (to seize, take, conceive) is made up of two words: *sun* (4862)
and *lambano* (2983). *Lambano* means to take or receive objectively. *Sun*
denotes union; with or together by companionship or process. The same
word is used in Luke 1:46: "And, behold, thy cousin Elisabeth, she hath
also *conceived* a son in her old age: and this is the sixth month with her,
who was called barren."

In Luke 35, the angel said, "holy spirit shall come upon thee."
"Come (1904)" and "upon (1909)" are the same words used in Acts
1:8a: "But ye shall receive (*lambano*) power (*dunamis,* 1411), [after
that] the holy spirit is *come upon* you." "Come (*eperchomai*)" means
to supervene and to arrive, and "upon (*epi*)" is a superimposition, as a
relation of distribution, rest, or direction. In this verse from Acts, Jesus
is instructing his Disciples as to what they should expect on the day of
Pentecost. The gift from the Holy Spirit *came upon* them just as it came
upon Mary, accompanied by the power needed to be "witnesses unto
the uttermost part of the earth."

In these two passages, the word "power (*dunamis*)" denotes the
inherent, miraculous, power of God, which shall "overshadow (*episkiazo,*
1982)" or cast shade upon. Every usage of the word *dunamis* in the Bible
is in relation to the power of God, whether in a cloud casting a shadow or
the shadow of Peter cast over people who desired healing.

While he yet spake, behold, a bright cloud *overshadowed* them:
and behold a voice out of the cloud, [which] said (saying), This
is my beloved Son, in whom I am well pleased; hear ye him.
(Mt 17:5)

YHWH said this is my beloved Son, my one and only.

> Insomuch that they brought forth the sick into the streets, and laid them on beds and couches, that at the least the shadow of Peter passing by might *overshadow* some of them. (Ac 5:15)

In order to gain a broader perspective on conception and birth in the Bible, let us consider other examples in the Word. The first regards to the birth of Samuel:

> And there was a certain man of Zorah, of the family of the Danites, whose name [was] Manoah; and his wife was barren, (*'aqar*, sterile) and bare (*yalad*) not. And the angel of the LORD, YHWH, appeared unto the woman, and said unto her, Behold now, thou art barren, and bearest not: *but* thou shalt *conceive* (*harah*, 2029) and bear a son. Now therefore beware, I pray thee, and drink not wine nor strong drink, and eat not any unclean thing: for, lo, thou shalt conceive (*harah*, become pregnant) and bear a son; and no rasor shall come on his head: for the child shall be a Nazarite unto God from the womb: and he shall begin to deliver Israel out of the hand of the Philistines. (Jdg 13:2–5)

A lot of mothers-to-be would do well to heed this advice: "drink not wine nor strong drink."

> And God said unto Abraham, As for Sarai thy wife, thou shalt not call her name Sarai, but Sarah shall her name be and I will bless her, and give thee a son also of her: yea, I will bless her, and she shall be [a mother] of nations; kings of people shall be of her. Then Abraham fell upon his face, and laughed, and said in his heart, Shall a child be born (*yalad*) unto him that is an hundred years old? and shall Sarah, that is ninety years old, bear (*yalad*)? (Ge 17:15–17)

> Now Abraham and Sarah [were] old [and] well stricken in age;
> it ceased to be with Sarah after the manner of women. Therefore
> Sarah laughed within herself, saying, After I am waxed old shall
> I have pleasure, my lord being old also? And the LORD said
> unto Abraham, Wherefore did Sarah laugh, saying, Shall I of
> a surety bear a child, which am old? Is any thing too hard for
> the LORD, YHWH? At the time appointed I will return unto
> thee, according to the time of life, and Sarah shall have a son.
> (Ge 18:11–14)

> And the LORD visited Sarah as he had said, and the LORD
> did unto Sarah as he had spoken. For Sarah *conceived* (*harah*)
> and bare (*yalad*) Abraham a son in his old age, at the set time of
> which God had spoken to him. (Ge 21:1–2)

> Through faith also Sara herself received (*lambano*) strength
> (*dunamis*) to conceive (*katabole*) seed (*sperma*) and *was delivered
> of a child when she was* past age, because she judged him faithful
> who had promised. (Heb 11:11)

The thought of Abraham and Sara having a child was "laughable" to
them. Sara could not imagine having that pleasure with Abraham. Sara was
incapable of having children and Manoah's wife was sterile. Abraham was
10 years older. These two examples demonstrate how nothing "is too hard
for YHWH" to accomplish. Here, God helped the situation along, so that
these two couples could have children of their own. This shows how far God
is willing to go to accomplish what He needs.

Prophesy of the Conception of Jesus Christ

Isaiah says this about Jesus' birth:

> Therefore the Lord himself shall give you a sign; Behold, a
> virgin shall *conceive*, and bear a son, and shall call his name
> Immanuel. Butter and honey shall he eat, *that he may know* to
> refuse the evil, and choose the good. For *before the child shall*

And almost all things are by the law purged with *blood*; and without shedding of blood is no remission. (Heb 9:22)

For the life of the flesh [is] in *the blood*: and I have given it to you upon the altar to make an atonement for your souls: for it [is] *the blood* [that] maketh an atonement for the soul. (Lev 17:11)

It is the blood that gives life to the flesh.

Forasmuch as ye know that ye were not redeemed with corruptible things, as silver and gold, from your vain conversation received by tradition from your fathers; but with *the precious blood* of Christ, *as of a lamb* without blemish and without spot. (1Pe 1:18–19)

God created the male side of the equation in the conception of Jesus Christ, the seed. The blood that ran through his veins was completely pure, precious. He had to be as much like Adam as possible to be the perfect sacrifice for our sin. Like Adam, he had the ability to sin, but chose not to. If he could not have sinned, then he was not flesh. Jesus probably looked a lot like Mary's father; after all, he did participate in her flesh. Conception could not have occurred without her egg, anymore than it could have without Sara's.

[Seeing] Then [that] we have a great high priest, that is passed into the heavens, Jesus *the* Son of God, let us hold fast [our] profession (or confession.) For we have not an high priest which cannot be touched with the feeling of our infirmities (weaknesses;) *but was in all points tempted* like as [we are, yet] without sin. (Heb 4:14–15)

Everyone knows that God cannot be tempted and He gives us the strength to resist temptation, just like He did Jesus. He was either temptible or he was not. The fact that he was, enables us to overcome temptations, like he did.

> Hereby know ye the spirit of God: Every spirit that confesseth [that] Jesus Christ is come (metaphorically, into being) in [the] flesh[13] is of God: and every spirit [that] confesseth not Jesus [Christ is come in the flesh] is not of God: and this is that [spirit] of antichrist, whereof ye have heard that it should come; and even now already is it in the world. Ye are of God, little children, and have overcome them: because greater is he [that is] in you, than he [that is] in the world. They are of the world: therefore speak they of the world, and the world heareth them. We are of God that knoweth God heareth us; that which is not of God heareth not us. Hereby know we *the spirit of truth*, and *the spirit of error*.[14] Beloved, let us love (*agapao*) one another: for love (*agape*) is of God; and every one that loveth is born of God, and knoweth God. He that loveth not knoweth not God; for God is love. In this was manifested the love of God toward us, because God sent[15] his only (*monogenes*) Son (ESV, GWT, NCV, WEB) into the world, that we might live through him. Herein is love, not that we loved God, but that he loved us, and sent his Son [to be the] propitiation (as atonement) for our sins. Beloved, if God so loved us, we ought also to love one another. No man hath seen God at any time (because He is spirit, which cannot be seen; not flesh, which can be). If we

---

[13] NT:4561 *sarx, sarkos, hee*; what can be stripped off from the bones; 1. properly, flesh (the soft substance of the living body, which covers the bones and is permeated with blood) of both men and beasts: 1 Co 15:39; 2. equivalent to the body; a. universally, Jn 6:63; b. used of natural or physical *origin*, generation, relationship: Ro 9:3. Thayer's

[14] NT:4106 *plane* (plan'-ay); feminine of NT:4108 (as abstractly); objectively, *fraudulence*; subjectively, a straying from orthodoxy or piety. NT:4108 *planos* (plan'-os); of uncertain affinity; roving (as a tramp), i.e. (by implication) *an impostor or misleader*; KJV - deceiver, seducing. Strong's

[15] NT:649 *apostello* (ap-os-tel'-lo); from NT:575 and NT:4724; set apart, i.e. (by implication) to send out (properly, on a mission) literally or figuratively. Strong's

Scripture Index

182

Printed in Great Britain
by Amazon

25818112R00118